CALIGULA

Borgo Press Books by ALEXANDRE DUMAS

Anthony
Caligula
The Count of Monte Cristo, Part One: The Betrayal of Edmond Dantès
The Count of Monte Cristo, Part Two: The Resurrection of Edmond Dantès
The Count of Monte Cristo, Part Three: The Rise of Monte Cristo
The Count of Monte Cristo, Part Four: The Revenge of Monte Cristo
A Fairy Tale (with Adolphe de Leuven and Léon Lhérie)
The Last of the Three Musketeers; or, The Prisoner of the Bastille (Musketeers #3)
The Three Musketeers—Twenty Years Later (Musketeers #2)
Napoléon Bonaparte
Richard Darlington (with Prosper Dinaux)
Sylvandire
The Three Musketeers (Musketeers #1)
The Two Dianas (with Paul Meurice)
Urbain Grandier and the Devils of Loudon
The Venetian
The Whites and the Blues
The Widow's Husband; and, Porthos in Search of an Outfit
Young Louix XIV

RELATED DRAMAS:

The Queen's Necklace, by Pierre Decourcelle
The San Felice, by Maurice Drack
The Son of Porthos the Musketeer, by Émile Blavet (Musketeers #4)
A Summer Night's Dream, by Adolphe de Leuven and Joseph-Bernard Rosier
The Widow's Husband; and, Porthos in Search of an Outfit: Two Dumasian Comedies, edited by Frank J. Morlock

CALIGULA

A PLAY IN FIVE ACTS

ALEXANDRE DUMAS

Translated and Adapted by Frank J. Morlock

THE BORGO PRESS
MMXII

CALIGULA

Copyright © 2000, 2012 by Frank J. Morlock

FIRST BORGO PRESS EDITION

Published by Wildside Press LLC

www.wildsidebooks.com

DEDICATION

To Conrad—

Yet another project that would never have seen the light of day without your support.

CONTENTS

CAST OF CHARACTERS 9

PROLOGUE 11

ACT I 55

ACT II 93

ACT III 127

ACT IV 149

ACT V 173

ABOUT THE AUTHOR 197

CAST OF CHARACTERS

Caligula

Claudius

Protogenus

Afranius

Cherea

Caius Lepidus

Annius Minucianus

Cornelius Sabinus

Aquila

Bibulus

Apelles

The City Praetor

A Lictor

A Soldier

A Porter

A Freedman

A Bath Attendant

Captain/Commander of the Praetorians

A Soldier

A Mendicant

A Slave

Messalina

Stella

Junia

Phoebe

Senators, Clients, Soldiers, Slaves, etc.

PROLOGUE

A street giving on the forum. A barber shop to the left front. On the door, the sign "Bibulus Barber." Further to the left, the Mansion of the Consul Afranius. Mid-stage on the right, a small house belonging to Messalina. In the middle, the Sacred Way giving on the Temples of Fortune and Jupiter the Destroyer. In the rear, the Tarpeian Rock.

Protogenus, two guards, and two slaves enter from the right crossing the stage and knocking on the door of the barber, Bibulus.

PROTOGENUS

Hola! Barber. Hola! Get up.

ONE OF THE GUARDS

The poor fellow is probably asleep dreaming how Jupiter Strator will give him his golden beard.

PROTOGENUS

More reason to wake him if he's in the midst of a sacrilegious dream. Hey! The door!

ONE OF THE GUARDS

(ready to rap with the pummel of his sword)

Shall I force it?

(Bibulus opens his window.)

PROTOGENUS

Lucky for him, eh?

BIBULUS

Sorry. I'm coming, Your Excellency.

(He shuts his window at the same moment Messalina's door opens and a Nubian slave pokes his head out and examines what's going on in the street.)

PROTOGENUS

As soon as he appears in the doorway, don't wait for him to come out—each of you seize his arm.

(Bibulus opens the door and is immediately pulled by the two guards.)

PROTOGENUS

Come here!

BIBULUS

Master! In the name of the gods what do you want here? I am a poor man, obscure. I have done nothing to enrage Caesar.

Consider, Masters, this cannot be.

PROTOGENUS

Caesar doesn't glance so low. He bears to heaven a face, radiant and superb—other eyes, look under the bushes for impure insects that vainly attempt to rise towards him to cause annoyance.

BIBULUS

(rapidly)

Yes, Caesar is a God! Jupiter is his father. Diana his wife and each knows that never by a mad or impious word would I dare to offend his divinity. I swear by Caesar and by his Sister Drusilla, that the emperor has no more docile slave than this poor barber who kneels before you and trembling, embraces your knees.

PROTOGENUS

There's nothing for you to fear at the moment.

BIBULUS

(rising)

Oh!

PROTOGENUS

No, but they tell me, friend, that your shop is always full of fashionable young men who require your talents—and the place has become the rendezvous of young insolents whose imprudent tongues in frivolous conversations criticize Caesar's words and deeds.

BIBULUS

And who in Rome would dare to speak imprudently of the divine Emperor?

PROTOGENUS

I don't know, but misfortune awaits those who have so much audacity! I will go into your house to establish myself in your place. My work is enhanced by luck. Today is the day of Caesar's triumph. I reason that on this occasion the crowd will form in the forum, avid for the spectacle. Around the milestone of gold, the center of the universe, all the many diverse populations will press. So, perhaps, in serving this confused mélange, I will stop some strange word in its flight. The type, they tell me, that sometimes echoes through your house in a low voice.

BIBULUS

Do as you will for Caesar is master. Caesar, like the Gods, enjoys the right to know everything. Caesar distinguishes crime from error. Hail Caesar! Caesar is a great emperor.

PROTOGENUS

Go!

(Protogenus enters Bibulus shop. The guards take Bibulus along. Protogenus shuts the door after himself.)

(The Nubian Slave who was watching from Messalina's house returns to the door.)

SLAVE

They are gone. The street is empty. Lord, you can go.

CHEREA

When, oh, my beauty, can I sleep between your cherished arms until dawn without worrying that some slave seated at our door to count the moments that pleasure brings us, will come to tell me when I awake an hour before dawn beside you. "Go young man, go—get up—time presses you. You must separate from your beautiful mistress for already in the east the morning star glows." Oh, when will I in my peaceful love, like a farm laborer with his agile scythe see the corn fall on top of itself, and not leave his field until it has been completely mowed?

Let heaven give me a joy unmixed. As it gives it to the ardent wine grower at his harvest who from morning to night gathers from his lost vine the ripe raisin hanging from its suspended face.

And will I never have this joy to which I aspire, like a fisherman whose boat is his empire, but who, so long as it pleases him, sails the bitter waves, and twenty times throws his nets into the sea?

Oh, this sweet leisure that man envies the gods, and that I would buy with ten years of my life. Goddess of my heart, oh! Tell me when fate will grant it to me?

MESSALINA

When Caesar is dead.

CHEREA

Oh, what! Always mixing bloody words with kisses suspended from our burning lips—and to make each moment shine in my view, in your eye vengeance, and in my hand the dagger. And you would do better, delight of my soul, to give yourself entirely to love—by which women rule—at the moment I were to do it for you. Oh, you should forget everything for me, who at a word from your cherished mouth, will leave his friends, relatives, life. My consular eagle and my old veterans, brothers who have seen me born and grow in their ranks! Do you want to change, fleeing this funereal Rome in a treasure of love. Which remains to us in the future? Leave your old husband and your royal lover. To sustain us, we can easily find some distant and profound retreat.

MESSALINA

Caesar extends his arm and touches the end of the world.

CHEREA

Caesar, always Caesar! He is returning today and I am going so that you may be better with him. Here are the thoughts which break, which torture, and render senseless those who suffer from them. Oh, you don't love me, cruel one, you who can leave me without dying—to share a single heart with two.

MESSALINA

Believe me, Caesar never consults my wishes. Caesar demanded my love or my life. He has obtained neither the one nor the other in his brutal desire—but in its place he has received a more fatal gift. And since that moment, his abused luxury has caressed my hate disguised as pleasure. You complain when you could avenge yourself, senseless one! Tribune, know the spot where a sword's point can open in the body a passage to the soul. Know that only by accomplishing my resolute plans will Olympus soon have one god the more. Caesar in heaven, there's nothing to fear on earth. No more terrors, no more. mysteries—no more coming between us to trouble our pleasures, except the ghost of a spouse without rights or desires, who left in a base orgy to sleep each night on a shameful table will never think, drunk until morning, to look for another bed other than the one of feasting. Then, my Cherea, no longer the importunate slave who troubles those few moments given us by Fortune, and who takes, before the hour (frightening our love) the light of the moon for the rays of day. Then to the mower—an unparalleled harvest. Then to the wine grower the treasurers of his wine. Then to the handsome fisherman who sails toward me: An ocean of love.

CHEREA

Very well, Caesar will die.

SLAVE

(running)

They are coming by the side door, reenter quickly, mistress.

MESSALINA

(pulled off by the slave)

Goodbye, my Cherea! I love you.

(She goes in.)

CHEREA

Enchantress. To deceive yourself in love is, they say, bad. I accept the challenge: That's fine, the more tricky, the better.

(Cherea hides by the door; Annius Minucianus, Cornelius Sabinus, Caius Lepidus enter crowned with flowers, their clothes messed up and laughing raucously.)

CHEREA

Who are these young fools?

ANNIUS

Let Cerberus take me off, if I don't see there, by a doorway something which takes human form.

SABINUS

Hey! Who goes there at night on the Roman highway?

LEPIDUS

It is to cut purses or to search for caresses—or do you come to steal our gold or our mistresses?

SABINUS

Your name, quickly, your name, for we are in a hurry.

CHEREA

Patience, lords. I don't know enough to answer you yet—who are you—I will tell you my name when I know yours.

LEPIDUS

That's very fair; and Minerva has spoken through your voice. Listen—the one you see to my right—or that you can't see for this miserly night is black enough to defy the mug of a Tartar—He's Annius, his father and mine used to be friends, moreover, republicans, I think—wait—yes, that's it. I pride myself on being precise. Do you know what the Republic was? Say it, if by chance you remember.

As for the rest, old Romans, more noble than Caesar and who descend right from the first stone which Deucalion threw behind him. This one now, who's on my left here—Where the deuce are you? Look, get over here—this other one who's hand is looking to touch mine—this is Sabinus, Praetorian, Tribune. I have to admit it; he's a new man. But he's elegant, the kind they call a dandy. He lisps while talking, puts on beauty spots, wears rouge. Which doesn't prevent him going to some ignoble pothouse with libertines, every night to play at dice and drinking wine. For the rest, full of spirit, but also some infamy, those who play the clown are adored by women. And whoever is a father, spouse or lover, must never take their eyes off them for a single moment. As for me, who portray them for you, I, your servant, who although Roman, wear Persian costume (for the reason, my dear fellow, that it is more elegant and keeps you warm in winter) my name is Lepidus, my father made me go to Athens more than 3 years ago with a pedagogue named Callisthenes and there I studied very hard. You see! But wisdom writes in nature and then in the immense work signed by Epicurus, I philosophized so long and so well, that I doubt everything and believe nothing—if it's not pleasant, except the divine flame—that Jupiter has put in wine and woman—beaten from a hurricane sent by the gods and the proof is that my professor drowned, day before yesterday, after I touched the port of Ostia to feast my return—we left to go together to the tavern for supper yesterday evening which being accomplished as you can see—we spent our nights with the most beautiful—with—the divine what's her name—some priests of Cybele makers of coffins, some Jews, some jugglers.

Still, Rome has the best thieves. In such a way that leaving the pothouse in good cheer we didn't want to go home to our hearth gods without beating up some night cohorts. That occupation has brought us here. So indeed finding ourselves near the shop of the barber Bibulus near the old forum, we decided to watch Caesar pass, who, this morning, dear fellow, by chance is triumphing.

Ah! Ah! Ah! How amusing life is and how Jupiter must have laughed when he created men.

And now, dear fellow, no longer having any more reasons to refuse to tell us your name, speak, as I have done: without fear or mystery.

CHEREA

You are mistaken, I must still be silent for you are not known well enough to me. And now that I know you better, I find my incognito necessary.

SABINUS

Oh! The joke changes its face. It has two faces like Janus—that's fine. One laughs, the other bites; man's face and dog's face.

CHEREA

Will you let me pass?

ANNIUS

The thing is impossible.

CHEREA

Take care!

SABINUS

(laughing)

Ah, ah, ah—his rage is laughable.

CHEREA

(drawing his sword)

Get back!

LEPIDUS

(to Annius)

What do you say to this threatening tone?

CHEREA

I told you I was going to pass and I prove it by passing.

(He slips between Annius and Lepidus.)

LEPIDUS

(falling in the arms or Annius who holds him)

What are you doing?

ANNIUS

(pointing to Cherea)

Cherea, the lover of Messalina.

LEPIDUS

That's another matter then. Before you I bow. You, who press happily such a rich treasure in your loving arms—I want to merit favors as great. At this door also hang garlands—and pour balm on this doorstep—and odorous myrrh—and perfume, yes, from tonight.

SABINUS

Excuse me! From the moment that the orgy degenerates into an idyll and turns into an elegy—then I want no more of it. Good day. Near here I know an honest place where one can gamble—and I am going there.

LEPIDUS

Do you have need of money?

SABINUS

Several thousand sesterces, resulting from my bartering a produce of my commerce—with a usurer, who, on pawn, my dear, lends me twenty per hundred. Huh! It's not very expensive for who knows what the interest rate is in Rome? I want to introduce you one day to this brave man. Where will I find you?

LEPIDUS

Here, at the barber's facing the object of my new ardor.

(exit Sabinus)

ANNIUS

Listen, Lepidus, of the three of us—without argument, the most drunk—it's me.

LEPIDUS

So be it.

ANNIUS

You want to live? You want to die? Choose!

LEPIDUS

Me?

ANNIUS

You!

LEPIDUS

Bad joke!

ANNIUS

Answer.

LEPIDUS

I much prefer to live.

ANNIUS

Then—let's get out of here.

LEPIDUS

Me? Go without seeing this divine woman?

ANNIUS

Fool, Who asks to see the Messalina! Oh, thrice fool!

LEPIDUS

Look, as in all places, merit brings the envious after it.

ANNIUS

Why don't you know who she is, this woman?

LEPIDUS

I know that her beautiful body incases a flaming heart—and that Cupid—to whom all fates are known gives her to be a priestess to his mother, Venus.

ANNIUS

Well, then, it is I who must tell you the rest. Listen: better for you to be like Orestes, having by an execrable, odious crime amassed on your head the rage of the gods than by some profane desire to have the devouring glance of that courtesan fall on you. Believe me, don't stop to extend your hand to ill luck which follows on the other side of the street. Fear this woman with somber eyes, pale lips who , they say, was on the fatal Ides. For do not think, child, that this love will be a joyous amour that sings in broad day. A love that, in the evening, as the resinous fire leads to your door the Tibicine Flute—and who weary with joy—wakens the day on a bed all covered with festive roses. Not so, friend! These are taciturn amours seeking strange and nocturnal voluptuaries who go from pleasure to pleasure which exhaust sometimes but never satisfy—which hide in the shadows leaving infamy in their path—some unknown body of a child, man or woman, for the Tiber already, accomplice to prudent waves, washes into the sea the head, a gag in its teeth. Believe me, don't tempt the plots she hatches. We have enough of tigers without she-wolves.

LEPIDUS

What are you saying?

ANNIUS

I tell you what everyone will whisper to you—or rather no, won't tell you. For none of us knows anything except that at first light the dawn opens its joyous eyelid—in that cursed prison cell or some pious tomb, the night, captive or dead, closes its eyes. So that one who knows the peril, if he confronts it, soon frees his most faithful slave and puts a short and discreet sword under his tunic, having without cease an assassin quite ready, who,—on the occasion, with a prompt and sure hand recognizing the executioner saves himself from torture. Yes, because we are incessantly spied on—spied on by the waves which wash over our feet, spied on by the birds which pass over our heads, spied on by the serpent which flees and leaves no trace, by the shrubs of the plain and the trees in the woods—all find a sound, a language, a voice to repeat to their wild masters the conspiracy that a dream murmured in our mouths. You doubt?

LEPIDUS

Yes.

ANNIUS

It's true. You will see.

LEPIDUS

Terror makes you crazy, my dear fellow—I really think the Emperor is sometimes disposed to make Rome tremble, but, in the end, the Emperor is a man born of a woman and who being born, like others is nourished on milk not blood. If he's a tiger, then he must be chained up.

ANNIUS

It's clear, poor fool, that you're just returned from Athens and you haven't seen, as we have, with your own eyes his wrath mount from men even to the gods. Yes, he was a child like other children—his soul opened to human feelings—but this woman by some dark design has poured in his cup a love potion which has rendered him senseless. So much so that it is no longer Caesar but Messalina who reigns on the Palatine, the royal hill! That's why you must doubly flee her glance. Incestuous mirror burning so that Caesar cannot see—blinded by the fire of her eye. Among all the lovers who fall before her Cherea alone remains—because she's attached to him and lets him live in some hidden place.

LEPIDUS

Well, so be it! Such advice my prudence foresaw—renounce her love but not her sight.

(Messalina's gate opens.)

ANNIUS

Heaven! your fatal desire is fulfilled. There's Messalina who is going to pass by. Look at her, I've done what I can. You are free to follow her.

(Messalina reclining on a litter of purple and golden flowers lit from the inside by a lantern with golden designs, carried by four slaves—of which the first two have collars and bridles of gold and preceded by a Nubian slave, enters.)

(Messalina crosses the stage.)

MESSALINA

How sweet this night is—and how it sweetens life.

(She leaves by the left.)

ANNIUS

She reenters the palace without inconvenience. That's well—the sun can now appear in the firmament.

(Protogenus in barber attire enters his shop—then the concierge of the house of Afranius. A beggar. People coming to ask for the dole—young Romans coming to be shaved, coiffured and depilitated.)

LEPIDUS

Now that I've completed my dream, Annius, shall we go wake up Bibulus?

ANNIUS

He's up already.

(Protegenus leaves the shop and has the two slaves raise the windbreaker—which is shut—with an iron chain. He comes toward the two young men.)

PROTOGENUS

Greetings, knights.

LEPIDUS

Good morning, master.

(to Annius)

Shall we go get a haircut?

ANNIUS

So be it.

PROTOGENUS

Masters, I am all yours. A moment only to put my shop in order.

(laughing)

Let's put the irons in the fire, that's the way to do things.

LEPIDUS

Do you want to tell me why such a crowd was here at the break of day?

ANNIUS

You see, they came to ask the dole of the noble Afranius, the consul.

LEPIDUS

By Hercules! Another whose exploits I search vainly for and whose name I hear for the first time. Who is this man? Is he a Moor? A Gaul? A Scythe? Has he fallen from heaven or risen from Hell? Has he a family, a father, ancestors?

ANNIUS

I really think he has. His relatives are gods—gods they must be for the honors he seeks. His father's name is Pride, his mother Intrigue.

(The Consul's Doorkeeper opens the gate and pushes back the crowd. He holds a purse in his hand.)

GATEKEEPER

Hola! Jokers! Hola—you're in a big hurry! Back off there, milord Poet—! Get back! You, pass. Pass, noble Cassius—you will find my master. As for you, wait till it pleases him to appear.

LEPIDUS

(continuing)

And how did he gain the consulate? Was it by debauchery or embezzlement? Did he sell his sister, prostitute his daughter—or loan money to the brother of Drusilla.

ANNIUS

No—better than all that. The noble Afranius, offered himself as a victim like Curtius!

LEPIDUS

As a victim?

ANNIUS

Yes, my dear, oh—it's quite a scandal—so funny, my word, that it is hard to believe.

LEPIDUS

Is it long?

ANNIUS

No.

LEPIDUS

Then tell it.

ANNIUS

The divine Emperor, Caesar Caligula was struck by an illness of which no one knew the cause. He was heading straight towards his apotheosis, and despite the honors that awaited him above, he appeared uneager to go to heaven quite so soon. So that, like the nymph Pyrene each courtier's eye changed to a fountain, and amongst all those eyes the ones which wept the most were those of the future consul, Afranius. So that seeing himself almost dissolving into a river, he cried, "Jupiter answer my prayer—take my days and for them give us those of Caesar." Whether the offering pleased Heaven or be it pure chance—or that the doctor, master of his sublime art had worried the victim, from this moment Caesar, who was marching toward death, suspended the voyage and returned to himself. So ravished was he to see the celestial light, that he made Afranius consul for his prayer.

(Enter Lictors.)

LEPIDUS

Isn't he going to leave? I notice the lictors.

ANNIUS

Yes, doubtless with the senator, he'll go to the temple with the Emperor to consult the auspices.

AFRANIUS

Romans, don't doubt it. The gods are propitious. Hurry to the temples—let joyous festoons hang from the columns and pediments. With golden armor dress the statues! Spread flowers and perfume through the streets. In our walls Caesar returns today as conqueror. Long live Caesar. Caesar is a great emperor.

(He leaves, followed by Lictors and clients.)

THE PEOPLE

Long live Caesar!

PROTOGENUS

Lords, are you ready?

LEPIDUS

Doubtless.

PROTOGENUS

Master, will you be seated?

LEPIDUS

Very willingly.

(pushing away the hand of a slave who wants to put a sheet

around his neck)

Bibulus give me the pincers and the mirror and I will depilate myself.

PROTOGENUS

Without a razor?

LEPIDUS

Without a razor.

(Protogenus gives them to him.)

LEPIDUS

This is very good.

PROTOGENUS

What type of coiffure do you intend to have, master?

LEPIDUS

I want it to fall in ringlets on my shoulder.

PROTOGENUS

(to a slave hair dresser)

You understand?

ANNIUS

Do you have the Daily Acts?

PROTOGENUS

(giving them to him)

Yes, Lord—

LEPIDUS

(pulling out hair)

That's very good—read it to us—it will distract us.

A BEGGAR

(holding a bowl in his hand)

(his head is shaved, he leans on a stick covered by bands—he wears a small picture representing a shipwreck on his neck hanging by a chain)

Master, I beg you to have some pity on a poor shipwrecked person who lived for six months after all his wealth was submerged near Cape Pachynum by a frightful storm which he only escaped by swimming and who wears on his neck—faithfully painted—the reproduction of that event.

BATHBOY

(shouting)

To the bath, Lord, to the bath.

BEGGAR

(shouting)

Oh, my master, oh!

LEPIDUS

(giving him a coin)

Here, joker.

BEGGAR

Some gold!

(kisses the coin)

ANNIUS

(reading the date of the Daily Acts)

January the 5th—already five days old!

PROTOGENUS

These are the latest.

LEPIDUS

Come on, read it anyway.

ANNIUS

(reading)

"Two twins were yesterday exposed at Velabri. A rich merchant coming from Calabria—and having no child—adopted them both."

LEPIDUS

The honest man.

ANNIUS

(continuing)

The banker Posthumous, after going bankrupt was surprised last night as he reached the great highway then taken to the urban Praetor and imprisoned.

LEPIDUS

Thief.

BATHBOY

To the bath, Milord, to the bath.

ANNIUS

(continuing)

"On the 21st of January, the day the Senate meets after the priests have offered sacrifice, Caesar, Imperator and all powerful lord, will return to Rome—"

LEPIDUS

This is interesting.

ANNIUS

"Conqueror of Britain and Germany—"

LEPIDUS

(looking at himself in the mirror)

By Jupiter, that's a strange mania because one is the son of a soldier, a warrior—to want in his turn to be covered with laurels. Wearing laurels was good for Caesar—bald to his neck—but not for Caius who wears a wig.

ANNIUS

(terrified)

Lepidus!

PROTOGENUS

(stopping him)

Not a word!

LEPIDUS

(still pulling out his beard)

Huh?

ANNIUS

Nothing.

LEPIDUS

Are you reading very low?

ANNIUS

No—I finished.

LEPIDUS

Why?

ANNIUS

Because I am tired.

LEPIDUS

Tired?

ANNIUS

Yes, tired! What more do you want me to say?

PROTOGENUS

(taking the manuscript)

My master, would it please you if I read in his place?

LEPIDUS

Surely, I intend to finish what I've begun.

(to Sabinus who enters)

By Hercules, my dear fellow, you come at a good time. We were resting for the ceremony.

PROTOGENUS

(reading)

"Conqueror of Britain and Germany bringing to decorate the temple of our gods—twenty chariots full of precious objects which he despoiled from the most distant shores—"

LEPIDUS

Four sacks of pebbles and sea shells.

PROTOGENUS

And bringing after him, like Germanicus, the proud children of the North chained and conquered.

LEPIDUS

Yes, we know that—it was after dinner, that Caesar gave this famous battle, where sixty Gauls disguised as Germans fell living into his valiant hands. Is that all?

PROTOGENUS

(going into his shop)

Yes, that's all.

BEGGAR

(rising and passing near Lepidus)

Take care of yourself, young man. There are more spies than paving stones in Rome.

ANNIUS

Flee, Lepidus, without losing another instant.

LEPIDUS

And why?

SABINUS

This barber is not Bibulus. It's some informer who impersonates him to disgrace us.

ANNIUS

Look, everyone has deserted the house of the accursed.

LEPIDUS

Why, you're afraid for nothing, my dear fellow—I haven't said anything.

ANNIUS

Said nothing! You just said enough in the times we live in to kill three men.

LEPIDUS

Have I compromised you?

SABINUS

No, not us, but yourself a great deal.

LEPIDUS

By Castor—there's nothing to fear for any but me.

ANNIUS

Only you!

LEPIDUS

In that case—

SABINUS

Flee!

LEPIDUS

Not at all—I'm staying.

ANNIUS

Oh what wretched and deadly blindness.

SABINUS

Think of it—it's not only death. It's torture.

LEPIDUS

Then I won't wait for it!

ANNIUS

Then you are going to flee!

SABINUS

I don't understand you anymore.

LEPIDUS

I—shall I chance running through plains and forests hunted by soldiers like a stag at bay, or like Marius in my nocturnal terrors bury myself alive in the swamps? I! Shall I give up one day to shorten my end by submitting to cold, heat, thirst and hunger? No—not at all!

ANNIUS

It's either torture or flight—

LEPIDUS

Isn't there a way to frustrate this pursuit? Speak!

SABINUS

I don't know of any.

LEPIDUS

Sabinus, your friendship blinds you to my fate. There is a way.

ANNIUS

Death—right?

LEPIDUS

So be it!

SABINUS

You—to die at your age? Impossible!

LEPIDUS

And why should I live longer? Man doesn't count the time that elapses, brothers, but only the days that are luminous and full. I've seen the pleasures of my ravished youth. So well that I've lived a long life. Let me then die, brothers, it is time—it's a blessing of the gods to die at 20 and not to feel in our young years the withering of the tarnished crowns on our foreheads. Today, if I shut my eyes I die candid and pure, still believing in the gods, in the joy of the home, in the sweet country, in consoling love—in cherished friendship—while, if I wait, despoiled of all wealth perhaps I would die believing in nothing. Then, faithful auditor of the master's words, from now on, at this time, I have a duty to submit. And that is well! For sooner than I hoped death comes for me, it finds me prepared. Anyway, why is death so much feared by men? A flight between Phoebus and the Earth where we are. If evil and good are born of feelings—at the same instant the feeling extinguishes man ceases to differentiate pleasure and pain he is free—from the gold or iron that was his chain—Death has nothing to take from resolute spirits. I am—it is not. It is, I am no more.

ANNIUS

Lepidus.

SABINUS

Brother.

LEPIDUS

Enough.

(making a sign to the bathboy)

Slave.

BATHBOY

Master?

LEPIDUS

Come here. Child, in a quiet room prepare a warm, voluptuous, perfumed bath—where one can sleep the sleep of those who are embalmed. Go.

(The slave goes out.)

SABINUS

You still intend to do it?

LEPIDUS

(taking his gold chain from his neck)

This chain is yours. It was the gift of a young and beautiful Athenian.

(to Annius)

This dagger is yours. When you need it, it is a faithful friend who will help you—now let us leave each other for my destiny is played out. The master said, death is a dreamless sleep".

Goodbye—I'm going to die!

ANNIUS

Oh Lepidus! Soon a god will avenge you.

LEPIDUS

(in the doorway)

I hope so—goodbye!

(He goes in. The two friends disappear into the crowd.)

THE PEOPLE

A courier! A courier!

AFRANIUS

(looking toward the courier)

Caesar's uncle! Place! Make way!

(Claudius enters dressed in a tunic without toga or cloak and carrying in his hand a letter covered with laurels.)

AFRANIUS

The noble Claudius!

CLAUDIUS

Himself—but for mercy's sake put your lictors in a circle and forbid these clamors.

AFRANIUS

(gestures to his lictors)

Surround us.

(to Claudius)

What's wrong with you?

CLAUDIUS

I'm dying of fatigue. Caesar (may the favor not prove fatal to me) chose me to bring this triumphal letter—another would have designated someone who could run, but I, who can hardly walk—oh—I may die of it!

AFRANIUS

(mysteriously)

No matter, Claudius, it was heaven that sent you.

CLAUDIUS

More like hell—this cursed roadway—it's so long—

AFRANIUS

(in a half voice)

The auguries are taken.

CLAUDIUS

What are they?

AFRANIUS

Unlucky!

CLAUDIUS

I am not surprised by that; they foretell my death.

AFRANIUS

Fear that the blow may strike much higher than you.

CLAUDIUS

Much higher? In that case little matter to me. But still—what are they?

AFRANIUS

Tonight in the heavens, soldiers were seen clashing noisily. A she-wolf has born its fruit—a shapeless mess—thunder radiated coming from right to left—in going to the altar the heifer bellowed. And when the sacrificer had with his reddened arms cut out the entrails with the sacred iron—in vain did he search for the heart. The same thing happened be it presage or chance when Great Caesar fell struck by Brutus.

CLAUDIUS

Well—what do you think of all this?

AFRANIUS

That Octavius never forgot the man who, first placed him on his way and had instructed him of the threatened peril, though he was only a slave, the one who falling on the steps of the throne made a crown roll at his feet! However, terrible an irritating warning it may be, can be seen in a happy light, for fatal to the sun whose course is run it becomes favorable to the rising star. What do you say about that, Claudius?

CLAUDIUS

Silence—let's speak low—these omens, consul—

AFRANIUS

Well—?

CLAUDIUS

I don't believe them. And now, goodbye, I've regained my strength.

(He continues on his way towards the capitol.)

AFRANIUS

(watching him go off)

The old fox has seen the trap under the bait. Fool that he is or that they say he is, I think that this man is even more farsighted than I am.

(A Decurion enters and lines his Praetorians from one side of the stage to the next.)

DECURION

Caesar. Hail Caesar!

(The lictors push the crowd back.)

LICTORS

It's the Emperor. Get back.

A LICTOR

(off stage)

Descend from your horse and you from your litter. On the ground both of you.

AQUILA

(in the wings)

Ill luck to you, Lictor. If your hand—

(Entering and noticing Afranius.)

AQUILA

Aren't you senator or consul?

AFRANIUS

I am consul.

AQUILA

Well—to you I protest.

AFRANIUS

What do you mean?

AQUILA

Your lictors insulted a woman. Consul—order them to let us pass.

AFRANIUS

Impossible, young man. No one can pass. Caesar is coming.

AQUILA

(aside)

It's true, on my word.

AFRANIUS

Do you see the messenger who is climbing to the capitol?

PEOPLE

Long live Caesar!

AQUILA

Yes—I see him.

(Making a movement to enter the wings.)

AQUILA

Stella, come see Caesar.

AFRANIUS

(stopping him)

By your long blond hair falling on your shoulders.

AQUILA

(excitedly)

My name is Aquila—I was born in Gaul—I have the rights of a citizen.

(taking Stella by the arm)

Come, my Stella.

STELLA

(veiled)

I'm afraid.

AQUILA

Come, then.

AFRANIUS

And this child?

AQUILA

She is Caesar's sister, if one can name sister, she who was nourished on the same milk as us.

AFRANIUS

And Rome is your country, young girl?

STELLA

Yes, Lord, but my mother lives at Baia. Do you know my mother, Junia?

AFRANIUS

Doubtless—and over Caesar she has total power.

STELLA

(raising her veil)

I came to find her again after five years of absence.

AFRANIUS

Approach then—Lictors, protect this child.

STELLA

Thanks!

PEOPLE

Long live Caesar! Conqueror. Triumphant!

PROTOGENUS

(entering in his own clothes)

Consul!

AFRANIUS

What? Oh, it's you.

PROTOGENUS

For a supreme order give me two lictors.

AFRANIUS

Take them.

(to Lictors)

Obey this friend of Caesar's as you would me—without hesitation.

(Protogenus takes the two lictors and with them enters the baths. The cortege begins to march by—soldiers bearing trophies enter first, then Incitatus, Caesar's war horse escorted by two Senators, then children crowned with roses who throw flowers—then finally, Caesar in an ivory and gold chariot drawn by four horses escorted by the hours of the day and night—behind the chariot the conquered prisoners—behind the prisoners, soldiers.)

THE HOURS OF THE DAY

(with gold palm leaves in their hands)

We are the warrior hours who preside over hard work when Bellona opens the barriers, when Caesar marches to the far shores. Our wild cohort shoots into the ardent throng. The stratagem that twists and turns. And over the field, vast tomb where bloody harvest falls we soar with the vultures smiling at this vast Hecatomb.

NIGHT HOURS

We are the happy hours by whom pleasure is escorted when

the amorous stars pierce the veil of night near the beauty who lies eye half opened, mouth half closed on a bed perfumed with roses. We guide Caesar and Cupid and then we live without truce to the moment when, as in a dream—the new born dawn carries us off in the first ray of day.

(A cloud descends and lowers itself near the chariot. Messalina appears as Victory a crown of gold in her hand.)

MESSALINA

And I Romans—I am faithful Victory whose powerful hand enchains luck—who braids for the conqueror the immortal crown and descends from heaven to crown Caesar.

CALIGULA

And now, o son of Mars and Rhea—people nourished on the milk of the sacred she-wolf—you can fight against all with impunity.

(he raises Messalina from her cloud and puts her near him on his chariot)

For Victory has taken Caesar for her lover!

(At this moment, Protogenus leaves preceded by a litter on which lies Lepidus covered by a cloak. His long hair can be seen hanging moist and the artery is still bleeding on one of his arms.)

SABINUS

(pointing at the cadaver to Annius)

Now is the time of brief agonies.

CALIGULA

To the Capitol! Children!

PROTOGENUS

Lictors—to the pillory.

PEOPLE

Long live Caesar!

STELLA

(frightened to Aquila)

Look!

ANNIUS and SABINUS

O—vengeance!

STELLA

Oh—terror!

PEOPLE

Long live Caesar! Caesar is a great Emperor.

(The two processions cross. The songs continue.)

CURTAIN

ACT I

An elegant room on the model of the house of the Faun at Pompeii. To the left in the forestage a vaulted recession containing the Lares—before the Lares a small altar—a bed in bronze—several pieces of ancient furniture. A door in the rear opens on the Tri Lurian. Two side doors.

JUNIA

(praying on the altar of her gods)

Familial penates, rustic divinities who watch over the joy of family life—who, protectors of the field, guardians of the house—defend them from theft and treason, if I have, each morning, crowned your heads, faithfully dressed the laurels and violets and if, each autumn I have offered on your altars the most beautiful of fruits, then O my paternal gods, deign to remember my holy piety and redouble your cares for this dwelling for, after a lengthy absence interrupting the mourning period my Stella will today cross the door sill. Do you remember this rebel child clearly? Didn't you find her beautiful with her sweet smile, with her face so pure and her eyes which reflected heavenly blue—and her hair drowning on her adored shoulder and raised by the wind like golden waves? Well, this child, grown and even more beautiful, this hope of my heart, this precious treasure, a mother in terror (agitated today by a vague Chimera) confides to you.

(Phoebe appears at the door escorting Stella and Aquila. She wants to advance toward Junia but Stella retains her and comes slowly with Aquila to a place behind her mother.)

If you guard her well, your cult will equal for me the cult of the great gods. Then at your altar, in addition to the gifts of barley and honey given by my servants, I will pour the purest wine from my wine room. I will sacrifices a ram to you every month. And then, ending the circle of a year, April will bring the joyous day to dawn when Lucina permits—To feast the birth of this girl, fruit of a chaste and tender love—with a white heifer. O my gods, you will be overwhelmed with sacrifices. But first quickly bring my Stella, I am thirsty to see her.

STELLA

Mother—here I am!

JUNIA

(throwing herself in Stella's arms)

My Stella, my child, my daughter—oh—yes—it's she!

(taking her hands and looking at her)

Oh! Let me see you—how big and beautiful she is!

STELLA

Mother!

JUNIA

Let me touch your long hair—do you want me to hug you again?

STELLA

If you want to! Forever, forever—

JUNIA

Child! Oh, how happy I am!

STELLA

And me, too, isn't absence frightful? Speak.

JUNIA

Don't speak about it anymore. I've found my treasure again.

STELLA

(showing Aquila to her mother)

And him, mother, and him—have you nothing to say to him?

JUNIA

(taking the hand of the young man)

Yes! Welcome—only son of my brother.

AQUILA

(bowing)

Oh, noble Junia!

JUNIA

Call me your mother!

AQUILA

My mother—how sweet it is to say that name.

JUNIA

Hasn't my son come to embrace me in his turn?

(in a low voice, holding him in her arms and pointing to her daughter)

Aquila, am I blind in my tenderness. Isn't she beautiful?

AQUILA

Oh, like a goddess.

JUNIA

My daughter, a good genius has watched over your days.

STELLA

(pointing to Aquila)

The good genius is there—protecting them forever. Oh, if you had seen him during this long trip, escorting my litter, separating all obstacles of whatever kind from my way.

JUNIA

He did the duty of a tender fiancé and his fear watched, prudent and jealous—a bit over my child, much over his spouse. Ah—those words makes you blush—come on—that's all right—we won't speak of it any more—let's sit down and talk about something else.

STELLA

(sitting)

This is my place.

JUNIA

Yes, your place, sweetheart. Wait.

(Showing her a work of knitting.)

JUNIA

Do you recognize it?

STELLA

What?

JUNIA

This is embroidery.

STELLA

It's a veil for you.

JUNIA

Look, it's lasted five years after being interrupted.

STELLA

I will finish it.

JUNIA

Have you indeed recognized all your family? Our old Geta who called you his daughter, this good Phoebe, who you called sister—and the dog painted on the wall, who caused you such fear? But, I'm always talking, you see—it's from delirium—your turn! You must have a hundred things to say to me. I am listening to you—go ahead.

STELLA

Yes mother, I have a great secret.

JUNIA

Really—my Stella, a secret. Speak then.

STELLA

First of all, O my dear mother, my name is no longer Stella—call me Mary.

JUNIA

What are you saying, my daughter—and how is it the name I gave you is no longer yours?

STELLA

(joining hands)

Pardon!

JUNIA

Mary!

STELLA

(with religious fervor)

Oh—it's the name of a sacred virgin.

JUNIA

But so is the other one—

STELLA

(interrupting her)

That an adored mother gave it to me I know—I want to keep it too—Let me leave both.

JUNIA

But where does it come from?

STELLA

Here—my good aunt, the mother of Aquila possessed a winter residence in Narbonne—but she also had a summer villa on the beach in a place called the camp of Marius—great pines covered it with shade and freshened the air, silent by day but when night came the sea spoke with an unknown language—and I used to be pleased to come to the shore to sit at night to catch the fresh breeze as the night clouded the humid plain. And bending over the immense mirror, I heard a voice both solemn and savage which I always yearned to understand. Then when

I'd tired for a long while, my jealous heart recalled my spirit to sweeter thoughts—I quietly questioned this intelligent wave which rolls from Sagenta to Agrigentum and I asked it if, in passing by Baiea it's waves had not seen my mother Junia?

JUNIA

Dear child.

STELLA

One night I stayed longer than usual in this solitude.

JUNIA

How could you expose yourself alone so, my Stella?

AQUILA

(smiling)

Oh, mother I wasn't far away.

STELLA

(continuing)

Then I saw coming a ship without pilot or oars—carrying two men and two women. And, unheard of spectacle which ravished me yet more, the four had haloes of gold over their heads from which escaped rays of bright light. I was obliged to lower my eyelids—and then I reopened them with fright—the divine voyagers were near me. One day I will tell you the story of each of them in all their glory. And you will adore them, I hope—for the moment, mother, all you need to know is that all four came from the depths of Syria. An edict banished them from their country. And acting as executioners, some irritated men put them to sea during a storm in a frail bark stranded on the shore, without oars, water, bread, and tied up. But hardly had the skiff touched the waves when at a song sung by the holy sailors, the storm folded its shivering wings and the sea smoothed its surging waves. And the sun reappeared in the heavens and enveloped the skiff in a radiant circle—!

JUNIA

Why, it was a prodigy!

STELLA

A miracle, mother! Their chains fell off by themselves. The water ceased to be bitter, and twice each day, the boat was covered by manna like that of the desert. So it was thus, pushed by a celestial hand I saw them land.

JUNIA

Oh—tell the rest quickly!

STELLA

At dawn, three of them left the house. Martha took the road which led to Tarascon—Lazarus and Maximum the way to Marseille. And she who remained was the prettiest. Toward mid-day we called to see if the mountains or the woods of the neighborhood were hiding some profound and silent retreat which could separate her forever from the world.

Aquila recalled that he had penetrated a savage cave ignored by all—a grotto crossing the flanks of the Alps where the eagle takes his air above the abyss.

He offered her this exile, and by the next day with both of us to guide her, we were on the road. The evening of the second day we touched base. There, falling on her knees in a holy ecstasy, she prayed a long while then, removing her sandals, she marched with naked feet toward the unknown cave.

Our cries and our prayers had no effect. In the midst of stones, thorns and brambles, we saw her mount, stick in hand and only at the end of the road did she fall without strength and without breath.

JUNIA

What was her name, daughter?

STELLA

Madeline, mother. This woman, insensible to sorrows, had dissipated the treasure of her youth among perfumes and flowers in the breast of pleasures condemned by heaven. But in her false pleasures, misfortune appeared. Her beloved brother, despite her cares—died. For the first time, prayer on her lips, she watched over the funeral couch, crying and shivering when suddenly she learned (from a man named John who came from Jordan, and who was soon going to leave, going to Samaria) of one called Jesus, son of Mary, a revered prophet that the people followed everywhere with love, shouting "Glory to God!"

For this man, being able to overcome obstacles, numbered his days for a long time with miracles. Madeleine was weak. She went to the port and falling on her knees said—"My brother is dead. Dead—and, if now you will it, his eyes although closed forever, will see light again—if your voice commands the seas, the winds—life or death."

Jesus said to her, "Come."

They went. Oh sadness! Already faithful hands had buried the mortal remains. Madeleine, weeping raised her arms to heaven, but the Savior said, "Woman do not cry." And marching toward the mean sepulcher, where Lazarus lay for eternity, Jesus, before the people immobile with fright, said, extending his hand, "Lazarus, rise!" Hardly had this protecting voice sounded when breaking the face of the marble tomb, Lazarus, obedient to the voice that called him, stood up in his tomb saying, "Here I am."

Then, at this spectacle, lost, breathless, joyous, and repentant at once, Madeleine ran towards her house and taking at random a precious vase, full of balm, she poured it over the knees of the prophet—then murmuring guilty confessions she humbled her head in the dust and dried his feet with her hair.

Then taking pity on her great distress, the Savior raised the holy sinner saying, "Much will be forgiven to you by an appeased God, O woman, having loved so much."

JUNIA

Doubtless they raise altars to this man?

STELLA

Mother, he was brought before the Roman Praetor—for he said aloud that the weak and the strong were equal before God, as before death. And while he could not express his thoughts in plain words, his parables pursued the powerful. The powerful were afraid! They said he was a false prophet! His death was resolved, and at their insistence a judge was found who pronounced sentence. But in the eyes of the Jews, assembled on Calvary, while the executioners in blind hate thought they were nailing his arms to a dirty cross, Mother, they were extending his hands to the whole world.

That's the divine man from whom I have received the law.

(falling to her knees)

If I've failed, mother, pardon me.

JUNIA

His law does not forbid you to love your mother?

STELLA

He makes it a pious and strict duty.

JUNIA

All law, which prescribes respect and love for those to whom they owe the light of day, O my daughter, believe me is a law of the soul. You cult has nothing for me to suspect or blame—and our pantheon is spacious enough to receive among our gods—a god the more. Doubtless my son has the same beliefs.

AQUILA

No, mother.

JUNIA

And why?

STELLA

(smiling)

It's that my science not yet being fully assured, I dare not, mother, press Aquila on this point. For it is only in leaving that

I felt running on my hair the holy water of Baptisms. Doubtless his turn will come—and my word, I am waiting for it. And God will inspire me when that time comes.

(Phoebe enters.)

JUNIA

What do you want with us, Phoebe?

PHOEBE

Mistress, a cohort of men and horses has stopped at our door.

JUNIA

(rising)

Some noble Roman who comes by chance to greet us in passing.

AQUILA

(who has looked)

Mother, it's Caesar.

STELLA

Oh, I am leaving.

JUNIA

And why, Stella, he's almost a brother?

STELLA

But they say he's bad?

JUNIA

No.

STELLA

No matter, mother.

JUNIA

As for me, I cannot believe this cruelty.

AQUILA

You nourished him.

STELLA

He's coming by this side.

JUNIA

Then go, my children.

(Aquila and Stella leave.)

JUNIA

(by the door at the rear)

Jupiter blesses me. Caesar in my home!

CALIGULA

Yes, myself, nurse. I am coming to Pouzzoli and being so near to Baiae, I wanted to greet my mother Junia. It's more than six months since I've seen her.

JUNIA

It's a god who gives me this unforeseen joy. But dare I still call my child one whom I see conqueror and triumphant?

CALIGULA

(lying on a couch)

You know of my battles against these barbaric peoples?

JUNIA

Caesar, renown has a hundred mouths.

CALIGULA

You flatter me, too.

JUNIA

I speak the truth.

CALIGULA

(stretching out)

Stop, nurse, be quiet, you've always spoiled me.

JUNIA

We were in great fear. The Master of Thunder—jealous they say of the god who reigns on earth wished to dethrone him. Judge our concern.

CALIGULA

Yes, like Theseus, I've seen somber shores and already the rock of Acheron avidly calls me with a great shout. But here's my Alcidas. To the gates of Teneriffe he came to find me. You know his vow?

JUNIA

I know that he's a name very dear—that Rome with a shout of profound piety told the province, and the province told the world. A name that made the name of Curtius pale, and this name, it's that of the noble Afranius. For the health of her son, the mother renders you thanks.

AFRANIUS

I have done what anyone would do in my place. Anyway, I had no great risk to run. Caesar is a god. Caesar cannot die!

CALIGULA

No matter, so many gods have visited Cerberus from the Divine Romulus to the Divine Tiberius, that before uttering a vow so hazardous, you have to look twice perhaps!

JUNIA

(pointing to Phoebe who brings a plate of wine and fruits)

Will Caesar do me the singular favor of drinking wine made from my vines and eating fruits gathered from my garden?

CALIGULA

Yes, but it seems to me that a more noble hand of cupbearer near mine ought to fill the office.

JUNIA

(taking the amphora)

That's very true!

CALIGULA

(stopping her)

What are you doing?

JUNIA

I am serving you.

CALIGULA

You, nurse!

JUNIA

My son wishes to deprive me of this sweet office?

CALIGULA

I would have thought it was a duty for my sister to pour, when I came to visit my mother. The hospitable wine in a brother's cup.

JUNIA

Ah! You know that she's just returned.

AFRANIUS

Doesn't Caesar know everything? Isn't Caesar a god?

JUNIA

Phoebe go find Stella for us.

(Phoebe exits.)

JUNIA

She's hardly crossed the sill of my door for an hour, and this day, my children, which sees you both return is a happy day indeed among my happy days. Wait—here she comes—look—how beautiful she is!

CALIGULA

And who is that who's coming with her?

JUNIA

It's our fiancée.

(Stella enters with Aquila and kneels.)

STELLA

May the gods protect you, Divine Caesar!

AQUILA

(bowing)

Hail, shining Emperor.

AFRANIUS

(low, to Caligula)

Well, did I deceive you?

CALIGULA

No—by my sister Drusilla!

(to Junia)

How have you been able to separate yourself from such a child for five years? Doubtless you gave so tender a mother, an absolute motive—tell me that, my sister?

STELLA

My mother's never told me the reason of this bitter separation. One day, I left her and since that day I've wept indeed—that's all I know.

JUNIA

(calling her daughter)

Stella!

CALIGULA

(smiling)

There, by Jupiter—some strange mysteries.

JUNIA

Stella—go pick the most beautiful oranges you can find.

CALIGULA

You're leaving?

JUNIA

For a moment. Go my daughter.

(Stella leaves.)

JUNIA

Caesar, you wanted to know how I was able to separate myself from this cherished flower? It was fear, alas that she would be ravaged! You remember, Tiberius in his last days when to rekindle his feeble amours the old tyrant of Capri by means of vile freedmen stole our daughters from the breasts of our families—Could I, in those times of misery and fear, imprudently keep your sister near me, fearing that, some evening, a furtive ship would kidnap my errant child from the shore? And that a wave would later return to me her cadaver, all scarred by the kisses of the infamous old man. But no longer being alarmed by such suspicions, for in case of danger, now she will have an all-powerful brother to protect her, right? I recalled my beloved child.

AQUILA

A Gaul takes on himself the case of protecting a mistress that he loves. And without the aid of anyone, I hope to keep the treasure which must belong to me.

JUNIA

(frightened)

Caesar will pardon these haughty words.

CALIGULA

Oh, I know the manners of my old Gauls. I love their rude speech—so reassure yourself. Besides your son-in-law is a brother of mine—O woman, leave us men to discourse on hunting and war—to your household chores.

(Junia leaves.)

CALIGULA

(turning to Aquila)

Well, my young Brennus, when the raging storm with its powerful voice scolds above to bow us down, do we stand resigned or do we always exchange blows with the lightning?

AQUILA

Always.

CALIGULA

And when the sea, gigantic lion, terrible and roaring in its rebellion cuts through our rocky barriers and senseless waves cover the shores—to punish its clarions and repulse its waves—shall we always hurl our javelins at it ?

AQUILA

Always.

CALIGULA

And if ever a second Alexander, Macedonian Phoenix reborn from his ashes asks you again what danger can make you tremble for your life—will you tell him always that you fear nothing, impassive athlete—if only heaven doesn't fall on your head ?

AQUILA

Always.

CALIGULA

And there's the bow in our familiar hands with whose darts we pierce the bear and the stag that we hunt in our ancient forests?

AQUILA

Alas, we no longer have our Druid forests. I was still an infant when one day there came a strange woodcutter from an ignorant country who with profane hands changed our woods into plains. Like corn he mowed our old oaks. They came, sent by an odious master to overturn our altars and proscribe our gods—and their hate, fertile in deadly examples, beat down the forests which served as Temples. Since that time, no, Caesar, alas no—there is no longer a huntsman who deserves the name for it's not hunting when a timid booby from a distance treacherously hurls a perfidious dart at a low flying eagle whose vermillion eye cannot see us from looking at the sun.

CALIGULA

During this scorned hunt your remarks seem, without doubt amusing—and your facile hand will surely send the arrow directly to where the eye guides it.

AQUILA

I think I've done it often enough to be certain.

CALIGULA

Give me then your proof.

AQUILA

(going to the door)

Caesar—don't you see on high, like a white spot a frightened swan pursued by a kite? Which of the two would you like me to hit?

CALIGULA

From so far?

AQUILA

Haste!

CALIGULA

The kite.

AQUILA

(looking and shooting)

Follow the arrow.

CALIGULA

By Castor—it's falling as it turns. Such a blow can't be believed unless seen. Go get it.

AQUILA

I am going.

(He leaves.)

CALIGULA

(quickly returning)

We are alone! Listen! By tomorrow, do you hear, by tomorrow—whatever it costs I must have that child.

AFRANIUS

Fine, Caesar—you shall have her. And the Gaul?

CALIGULA

Do with him whatever you wish.

STELLA

(bringing a basket of fruit)

Caesar, at the moment our orchards are barren.

CALIGULA

(pointing to the oranges)

But here are golden fruits from the field of the Hesperides.

JUNIA

This field is, alas, badly guarded by the dragon.

AQUILA

(entering and throwing at Caesar's feet, the kite pierced by an arrow)

Here—there is the kite you asked of me.

CALIGULA

That's fine.

(taking a cup)

Pour, mother. To your love, young man.

(He drinks and passes the cup to Aquila.)

AQUILA

Thanks Caesar.

(drinking)

STELLA

(offering the basket)

A fruit?

CALIGULA

Yes, I take this apple. But, like the shepherd Venus made a god—only to make it more beautiful. Goodbye.

JUNIA

Goodbye, Consul—goodbye my noble son. I hope we will see you again at Baiae.

CALIGULA

Yes, mother.

AQUILA

Hail, Caesar.

STELLA

Hail.

(Night begins to fall. Caligula and Afranius exit.)

JUNIA

Well, child are you still terrified of the emperor?

STELLA

No, mother. Caesar seems good, Caesar loves you—how can I not love him, myself?

JUNIA

And you, my son?

AQUILA

Caesar has respected our laws. Caesar has never harmed the Gauls. May the Gods keep Caesar from sorrow and trouble.

JUNIA

Fine! My son has, I believe, citizenship from a Roman city.

AQUILA

I was born to Latin rights—but having for a long while filled important posts I have the rank of citizen.

JUNIA

You know it's the custom in this case, every time one completes a voyage to go to the Urban Praetor, the same day to confirm arrival or return—the Praetor Lentulus lives not far from here—for this act, it barely requires a quarter of an hour—go then, my children—return soon.

AQUILA

Don't worry, mother.

JUNIA

(embracing her daughter)

Till later.

STELLA

Soon.

(Stella and Aquila exit. Phoebe enters with a large candelabra.)

JUNIA

Phoebe!

PHOEBE

Mistress?

JUNIA

Come. Have you repaired the disorder according to my command?

PHOEBE

I did it.

JUNIA

The perfumes.

PHOEBE

Prepared.

JUNIA

The baths?

PHOEBE

Heated—and whenever you wish, without fear of delay you can go there.

JUNIA

(shivering)

What? Don't you—

(listening)

Nothing, I thought I heard some shouts. Tell me, Stella's room— is it? Listen?

PHOEBE

Which way?

JUNIA

(pointing to the side by which her children left)

Over there!

PHOEBE

Nothing.

JUNIA

No—have you chosen her favorite room and poured perfumed oil into the golden lamp?

PHOEBE

Yes, myself.

AQUILA

(in the distance)

Mother!

JUNIA

Ah! This time I'm running there! A plaintive voice calls for help. You see, it was not a vain chimera!

AQUILA

(a bit closer)

Mother!

JUNIA

(rushing towards the door)

It's Aquila's voice! Come!

(Aquila, sword in hand, clothes in disorder and full of blood, rushes in meeting Junia at the door.)

AQUILA

Mother!

JUNIA

(recoiling shocked)

What have you done with Stella?

AQUILA

(choking)

Some brigands!

JUNIA

Shame on you! You have poorly defended her!

AQUILA

(pointing to his wounds)

Oh! Why look at me!

JUNIA

Blood.

AQUILA

(decidedly)

Mine.

JUNIA

Wounded?

AQUILA

What's the matter?

JUNIA

But my daughter.

AQUILA

There were ten of them. Listen, rouse your family, let's arm and run—oh! I will catch them, Mother, and by heaven, yes! I'll return her to you.

JUNIA

(distracted)

Yes, you said it—that's right—let's arm and get ready—slaves, servants—let's all run.

(The Urban Praetor, Protogenus and the two witnesses appear at the door—they are followed by lictors.)

PRAETOR

Stop!

JUNIA

What do you want?

AQUILA

It's yet another betrayal.

JUNIA

To me, my servants.

PRAETOR

Silence! Woman, you have just received this very day in your house a Gallic slave that his master reclaims.

JUNIA

You are mistaken.

PRAETOR

Enough.

JUNIA

No fugitive—

PRAETOR

(calling)

Hola!

JUNIA

Come here, I tell you.

PROTOGENUS

(comes forward and points to Aquila)

You lie—for there he is.

AQUILA

Me—a slave?

PROTOGENUS

You.

AQUILA

Me?

PROTOGENUS

You dare to disown me, your master?

AQUILA

You? You?

PROTOGENUS

Myself.

AQUILA

You, my master! Praetor, this man is mad!

PROTOGENUS

Praetor, I have my witnesses.

JUNIA

But he's my son.

PRAETOR

Silence.

JUNIA

At least listen to me.

PRAETOR

(to witnesses)

Come forward!

AQUILA

(grabbing them)

That's it—let's look each other in the face. You recognize me?

FIRST WITNESS

Yes.

AQUILA

You say?

JUNIA

Mercy—they are deceiving you, Praetor—a single moment—

AQUILA

You recognize me—me?

FIRST WITNESS

Perfectly.

PRAETOR

(presenting two stones to the witnesses which he has picked up from the courtyard)

Swear!

FIRST WITNESS

By Jupiter—by the Divine Augustus, I swear that the demand is just.

(pointing to Aquila)

And that I recognize this man.

(pointing to Protogenus)

That bought and paid for him—if I lie may Jupiter hurl me as far from him as I hurl this stone.

(throwing the stone behind him)

PRAETOR

(to send witness)

Do you swear likewise?

SECOND WITNESS

I do.

AQUILA

(annihilated and letting his sword fall)

Imposters!

PRAETOR

All is said, Lictors lead away this slave.

(The lictors take Aquila away and all leave except Junia.)

JUNIA

(alone)

Alone! Aquila—Stella! Alone—oh! Barren fate has taken all. This house like my heart is empty! And this in front of me! This before my eyes. In the domestic hearth—at the altar of my gods—still crowned with flowers which I braided when I prayed to them! Senseless prayers!

(marching towards the gods)

Who took your strength, who blinded you that you have not seen what happened? Or that having seen it, you did not let lightning fall on them to reduce them to powder? In what times are we living? And our times are odious, changed by mortals are they for the gods? O vain idols! When you were of clay, a mother could confide her daughter to you. You would guard the treasure of her virginity.

(putting her hand on them)

But, since they make you of bronze, of marble, of gold, sterile defenders, decorated egoists, you take care only to protect yourselves—when treason comes, you avert your eyes.

(breaking them and trampling them underfoot)

Be annihilated! You are false gods!

CURTAIN

ACT II

A terrace of the palace of Caesar on the Palatine Hill. It is surrounded by a gallery running on the outside with a colonnade. It is hung with material in the manner of a velum in a theater. Two side doors—a door in the rear giving on a floor and showing the top of a turning stairway—to the spectator's right a bronze bed. To the left, a table with a cedar box. At rise, a terrible storm rages.

CALIGULA

(clinging to two slaves)

Slaves, stay while this horrible storm roars over my head. Until the last lightning flashes remain—don't leave this place on your lives. It's the master of heaven whose jealous rage is directing this frightful storm against me. O Jupiter—Thunderer! Appease your wrath. I am not god. Lightning! On your knees! Yet one more blow which passes without striking me.

SLAVE

Master, the storm is passing. You have nothing to fear.

CALIGULA

Do you speak the truth? By the gods, protectors of oaths, I swear to free you, your wife.

(thunder)

You are lying.

SLAVE

Caesar can see the storm is passing off.

CALIGULA

Ah, yes, it's true. Listen Jupiter, I intend, like Augustus to found a temple to you.

(lightning)

Wait—! That will be made of—

(thunder)

Again! columns of bronze with capitals of gold. The storm is finally diminishing and I can breathe. I am still Caesar, the arbiter of the Empire, the Sovereign Master—all powerful in all places before whom Rome trembles, and whom they call god.

Ah—the lightning—frightened has fled before my glory—and vanquished Jupiter has ceded me the victory.

Go—and no one remain in error believing Caesar is a man or that Caesar was afraid.

(The slaves exit. Protogenus enters.)

PROTOGENUS

Be tranquil, Caesar, neither torture nor the rack will get anything out of them.

CALIGULA

Ah, it's you Protogenus, do you believe the storm is completely over?

PROTOGENUS

Yes, the last of flash from heaven is erased—Jupiter delivers us from all present danger.

CALIGULA

Let's not think of it any more then and let's revive ourselves. Well—have we succeeded in the enterprise?

PROTOGENUS

Yes.

CALIGULA

The white dove?

PROTOGENUS

She ought to be here.

CALIGULA

And our ardent Gaul was he put in shackles?

PROTOGENUS

Tonight he'll be escorted to the slave market.

CALIGULA

Good, I'm still the master of destiny.

PROTOGENUS

Could Caesar doubt it? In fact, Caesar is pale this morning.

CALIGULA

A dream, following this storm.

PROTOGENUS

Caesar knows every dream is an omen.

CALIGULA

By Drusilla—whoever can find a meaning in mine is a great magician.

PROTOGENUS

Caesar has sometimes tested my science. Does he wish to do so again?

CALIGULA

So be it! Hear me then—Serene and radiant, I was seated in heaven near the master of the gods when suddenly he turned an austere face towards me. And pushing me with his foot hurled me to the earth. I felt myself passing from Olympus to

Nothingness, then I was rolling on the shores of the ocean—the ebb tides brought the waves far from the shore, but then the tides came and changing color advanced going from green to the hue of blood. I wanted to flee, but weak as if after an orgy, I was soon caught by this red sea which passing the limit set for its waters enveloped my feet and its thousand traces, and sure that I was enchained on the beach continued to invade the coast. Now, seeing myself submerged by the waves, I called for help not thinking to swim. Then a voice disembodied, frightening, mysterious responded to my shouts—ordering me to be silent. I obeyed and all was reduced to silence for this tide made no noise as it rolled and swelled so much that my breast began to choke under the marine wave. I hoped the sea would cease to rise when—new prodigy—terrible to describe each wave rose on the bloody plain—and at its red summit bore a human head—and those heads were ones whose days I had cut off—the sea kept rising! I saw pass before me on the abyss from Antonia my first victim right up to Cassius Longinus dead yesterday whom the oracle told me to beware of—each head uttering from its pale mouth a name that I knew as well as the head itself. This lasted a long while, for our dead are numerous! Then, awakening from this frightful slumber, out of breath, my eyes haggard—I rose from my bed and found the hurricane continuing my dream. Dismayed by this double omen. I fled mixing together dream and reality until dawn, enemy of lies, took away the storm and the idea together.

PROTOGENUS

Caesar, you mustn't be forgetful of oneself or neglect the advice sent by the gods—In Rome, at this moment, something is preparing which resembles your thoughts as much as the tempest.

CALIGULA

And what's that?

PROTOGENUS

Wheat is lacking in our granaries.

CALIGULA

Wheat?

PROTOGENUS

Yes, Caesar, and yesterday evening the people having learned this baneful news gathered and forced the warehouses to pillage the rest.

CALIGULA

And how can the wheat be lacking?

PROTOGENUS

Why? Because throughout Italy, at this time—where our nourishing wheat grew are planted palaces and regal houses so that a day will come when palaces and regal houses will have crushed the harvests under their marble feet. And we need to find other countries' fertile fields so as to twice a year nourish our golden famines, which no sooner done, preventing the approach, a capricious wind keeps from port, the fleet from Sicily or even Alexandria—pushing the fleet back in fury towards the sea. Then with its granaries soon empty, all Latium, like a single man, is hungry—and like a beggar comes to demand alms of Caesar, Emperor and Prefect of—

CALIGULA

Fine! Like a beggar insensible to insult let them come—! And beneath my foot I will push down their face for I am weary of seeing this insatiable people, incessantly nourished by crumbs from my table. And since they're too proud to harvest their bread and they lack wheat—so much the better. They'll starve. Didn't a Prophet, who reads the stars, come to me to announce other disasters for them? For I hate them so much that I'd give a lot for them to have but one head to cut off.

PROTOGENUS

Caesar doesn't with to stop the course of rebellion while it is weak at it's source?

CALIGULA

No—let it emerge from its obscure abode. And when in broad daylight its wave bursts forth, we will force it, indeed to regain its shore. Then we will chastise it with our bold whips. As Xeres did to the Hellespont formerly. The danger isn't from those I suspect.

PROTOGENUS

Caesar wishes to know the names of the chiefs?

CALIGULA

Doubtless—but there must be many to lead this dangerous project to its end.

PROTOGENUS

No—there are only two.

CALIGULA

(smiling with scorn)

We'll see.

PROTOGENUS

Annius is the first—his nobility goes back to the first days of Rome. The second is Sabinus, a tribune, I believe a man without lineage.

CALIGULA

Marvelous! Open this box and take out the books it contains. Tomorrow both their days will be terminated. And this end, once fixed, will not be delayed.

PROTOGENUS

(pulling from the drawer two books on which are written titles in letters of golden bronze)

Does Caesar wish the Sword or the Dagger?

CALIGULA

The Sword.

(taking a quill and dipping it in ink, writing)

Let's reserve the dagger which must be disguised for those I do the honor to fear—it's a luxury to pay to assassinate such heroes when one has an executioner.

PROTOGENUS

Caesar knows the depth of Roman virtue.

CALIGULA

Take the Praetorians and the German guards and by the tunnels bring them here—into the vaulted cellars that are under the palace. Take special care that no one see them—Now for Claudius—

PROTOGENUS

You wish—?

CALIGULA

Have him sent to me. I need a great thinker to advise me—then it pleases me to have my successor when I am straightening out such business not far from my eyes and near my ears.

PROTOGENUS

And Messalina?

CALIGULA

What of her?

PROTOGENUS

Do you wish to see her, too?

CALIGULA

Don't worry—she knows the way here. And perhaps already

our beautiful captive arrives with Afranius this morning.

PROTOGENUS

By the way, I was forgetting—your Doctor Cneus went to the Praetor to cite Afranius.

CALIGULA

For what cause?

PROTOGENUS

In the very just cause that he pay thirty talents of good money which he promised for learning the instant that, without risk, he could dedicate his head to Caesar.

CALIGULA

That's fine—thanks.

(The door opens. Afranius appears.)

AFRANIUS

Caesar.

CALIGULA

Just our man! Hail, consul.

AFRANIUS

Does Caesar have the apple ready?

CALIGULA

Has the goddess Venus already come?

AFRANIUS

Yes, Caesar, she's waiting.

CALIGULA

Fine: Let her come.

AFRANIUS

(calling a slave)

Hola!

(giving order to him very low)

CALIGULA

(to Protogenus)

Go by Claudius' on return from the barracks.

PROTOGENUS

And if he's missing from the palace?

CALIGULA

Look for him in the taverns.

(He makes Protogenus leave by the door at right.)

AFRANIUS

(approaching)

Caesar will not forget that it is I, who—

CALIGULA

No, truly, and Caesar knows the price devotion is worth.

AFRANIUS

Which way does Caesar wish me to leave so as not to meet Stella?

CALIGULA

(escorting him to the door at left)

Through this door. Goodbye Consul.

AFRANIUS

Caesar has nothing further to command? Anyway, I'll return.

CALIGULA

Caesar hopes so indeed.

(Afranius leaves.)

CALIGULA

(alone)

Go—and now come, oh my beautiful blonde—come, for Caesar

awaits you—Caesar—-master of the world, Caesar whom the people implore for their lives, and who replies "Much later! I'm busy with my love life." Yes, from my bed, I love to see this slavish people rumble like a volcano and spread its lava—for it rocks my pleasures with its tremors and if I wish to sleep, then I say "enough". Yes, I love to think that the ardent jealousy of Messalina is prowling around me in its frenzy—Messalina whose eye is dark and piercing, whose fiery mouth wounds with kisses—so that I intend to torture her someday—to learn from her where this strangely faithful love comes from that leaves me to sometimes find other amours but whose charms always recapture me.

Yes, that's what my jaded spirits need to descend on my heart—rosy storms, scoldings, jealous, transports! Roaring, rebellion to serve as a concert at the pleasures of a lion!

(Caligula is seated. Two men escort Stella in.)

STELLA

Where am I, and why have you kidnapped me? What is this palace?

(noticing Caesar)

Ah! Caesar!

(running to him and falling to her knees)

I am saved!

(those who have brought her exit)

Caesar—you don't know that people have taken me from my mother—beating Aquila—and that they wouldn't turn back despite my sad and constant prayer. Ah—they are evil people who respect nothing—and you will punish them.

CALIGULA

I will take good care of them.

STELLA

What! You can tolerate such disorder? Caesar—what they did—

CALIGULA

They did by my order. They had a mission to escort you here. And I would punish them if they didn't succeed. I love you and wanted to see you again dead or alive. That astonishes you, child?

STELLA

Oh, that appalls me!

CALIGULA

This is the way I treat my good Romans. Are you unaware of it? Why did Jupiter put in my hands supreme power except so that I may do what he himself does?

Do you alone wish to deny the gifts he accorded me? Come on, sweeten up—come my beautiful Leda. I know that you follow the austere route by way of virtues, but a god can free you of your earthly yoke. Don't repulse your divine ravisher.

STELLA

Caesar, don't forget that I am your sister.

CALIGULA

Eh! Why, on the contrary, it seems to me I remember it—and I was, at all times, a quite excellent brother.

My three sisters have been my wives each in their turn. And as for Drusilla, everyone knows she was my lover—and when she died, I ran like a madman throughout the Campagna—compelled by a dark spirit—and that since that day, when I take an oath, I constantly swear by her divinity. Well, I will love you as I loved Drusilla—but the complacent gods and docile destiny will, I hope, give us a longer relationship.

(surrounding her in his arms)

Come, my beloved.

STELLA

(lowering her veil and crossing her two arms over her breasts)

Help me, holy modesty. On my blushing face come thicken my veil.

CALIGULA

This tissue is too thin to hide a star. And then, you seem to misunderstand that in these times that the love of Caesar is not like other loves, happy to wait at leisure for what is given him—and that force comes to his aid in the case of a refusal where he would bear an affront—sword in hand—crown on head.

Child, don't indulge in scorn any longer. And think, in time, where you are going—you will be broken to pieces—

For your arm is weak and mine is strong and that if I wish to, without effort—

(lifting off her veil)

—tear it from your face to see freely the features it hides from me—Chaldean, renowned for my enchantments, I can make these frivolous dresses fall. And, if in my vengeance, a soft word doesn't stop me—I can make your head fall off as easily.

STELLA

(falling on her knees)

Oh, my God, give me the strength to suffer—and forgive my death to him who makes me die.

CALIGULA

(raising her)

Well, then—

JUNIA

(behind the door at the rear)

I tell you that I am dear to Caesar and may enter at any time.

STELLA

(wanting to rush to the door)

Oh—my mother!

(Caligula stops her and puts his hand over her mouth.)

STELLA

My mother!

CALIGULA

(pulling her toward the door at the right, opening it and entrusting Stella to some slaves)

Take this child and watch over her. You will answer for everything with your head. Go!

(They take Stella away.)

CALIGULA

(running to the door at back where Junia is knocking and opening it himself)

Why didn't you open? Pardon me, nurse, I recognize your voice. What do you want with me?

JUNIA

Justice! They took my child, they stole your sister from me, Caesar!

CALIGULA

And you know the infamous ravisher?

JUNIA

No, but I come to you, face covered with dust—to you, the all-powerful, to you who hold the lightning, to you, my son—to you who, like a God, knows everything—to ask my daughter back. Right now, in every place your imperial army can freely search. Caesar, give me my Stella, my daughter, my child and truly you will be a triumphant Emperor—who with one hand strikes the enemy like a man, and with the other dries the tears of Rome.

CALIGULA

But mother, how shall I know where to find her?

JUNIA

Listen to me, let's not lose time. Come! I will go before you. Instinct will guide me, noble son of Agrippina as it guided Ceres following Prosperina. And as she lit two torches, one after the other, to search for my Stella at night, as if it were day—I will go without resting in my bitter sorrows—on my route with great shouts—questioning mothers and following all ways which they offer me even if it were to take me to Hell.

CALIGULA

But Aquila can help us in this task.

JUNIA

Ah, how a mother's love is egotistic and cowardly. I didn't tell you. I forgot about him. They've taken him as a slave—beaten, taken, chained him. Escorted him, I don't know where! You see quite well that it is right for you, Caesar, for you, the grandson of Augustus to punish without delay two crimes committed near you, before your eyes. And it cannot be that your sister is outraged, made to blush by an affront and for her not to be avenged.

CALIGULA

Then you are accusing some noble Roman?

JUNIA

No, I felt the iron but I did not see the hand. But, in advance there are those known—that ought to be suspected of a rape or perjury—more than one around you is an old offender. Your uncle—

CALIGULA

Claudius?

JUNIA

Yes, yes—him above all.

CALIGULA

(with scorn)

You do him too much honor when you condemn him. Claudius needs base courtesans that's all.

JUNIA

Cherea perhaps could be suspect.

CALIGULA

(skeptical)

The crime is very weighty for an effeminate, who, sleeping on flowers drinks to Venus ceaselessly in a cup of gold heavier than his sword—

JUNIA

Sabinus.

CALIGULA

(smiling)

That one, nurse, for the moment is occupied with the success of a more important project. He's conspiring.

JUNIA

Bad luck!

CALIGULA

Now, listen, the culprit is a noble— doubtless a powerful man—who could, fearing to see his crimes exposed extend his desperate blows even against you.

JUNIA

So be it! He has made my life bitter—not my death.

CALIGULA

But I, I must watch over the life of my mother, you shan't leave. I intend from this moment to lodge you in the palace, in an apartment where for fear of an un-foreseen plot harming you, my most trusted soldiers will keep you from sight. As for my sister, I will find her.

JUNIA

Oh—I love you, my son—but I will adore you like a God! Don't lose a day, an hour!

CALIGULA

If I lose an instant, mother, may I die! Caesar does not promise vainly—from my hand you will receive your daughter back.

JUNIA

When?

CALIGULA

Tomorrow.

JUNIA

Oh, my son, my Caesar, my emperor, my master—with this word tomorrow, you make me submit. Where must I go? Escort me, here I am—Oh—tomorrow did you say? Tomorrow?

CALIGULA

Yes.

JUNIA

(trembling at the noise of the people who have begun to assemble at the foot of the palace)

What's that?

CALIGULA

Nothing. Reality is only following the dream.

JUNIA

This ruckus?

CALIGULA

It's the ocean washing up on the beach but from here we can foil its plots.

(knocking with his feet)

And this rock, mother, is the test of its waves.

(They leave by the door at the rear—at the same moment Messalina raises the tapestry of the door on the left and follows them with her eyes.)

MESSALINA

(alone)

Fine! Carefully separate the girl from her mother—place a strict guard over every door—despite the separation and the soldiers and you, I'll go to them if I choose. By Venus, Caesar conspires against himself and the people are ready for another. Oh—the Empire, the Empire to which the world brings its tribute—with an Emperor like Claudius—that is to say with a cloak to conceal our shoulder, that is to say an actor given a bad role, who lets us rummage as we wish in this mine of gold named power! Oh—ill luck to the dragon that guards this new garden of the Hesperides from my hands, who at the entrance permits me to catch a glimpse of its fruits of gold and yet tries to prevent me from reaching my treasure! From instinct you vainly rise up against me, Serpent of pleasure. One day, by my caresses I will only have to press the weakened cords and I will stuff you in my thousand coils.

CALIGULA

(returning)

I am astonished not to have seen you already.

MESSALINA

I knew Caesar had a tender interview and I didn't wish—in such a sweet moment to distract the emperor with my—

CALIGULA

This morning we are in a very complacent mood. Watch yourself!

MESSALINA

My Jupiter jests—he imitates the God whose name he has taken and I shall no longer be prouder than Juno.

CALIGULA

O woman, to be changeable and restless like the tide!

MESSALINA

Well, what says Caesar of this beautiful blonde? Were her blue eyes so fatally powerful as to make him forget black eyes forever? These woman, they say, are of the languishing grace whose charm is powerful to amorous souls. Is Caesar seduced by these tame ardors?

CALIGULA

If Caesar is seduced it is only by tears.

MESSALINA

What! The innocent has already shed tears? Oh! How well we know all our charms, and how much sweeter than the sweet oriental—is a face at once weeping and smiling.

CALIGULA

It was a bitter sadness, and a real refusal, I am sure of it.

MESSALINA

Chimera! If Caesar had born the affront of her refusal, the audacious child would no longer be living.

CALIGULA

Ah! That's how Juno, in her rage, forgot what empire holds us and what law binds us. And that all impudence escapes the blow it deserves so long as it can wear the headbands of Vesta.

MESSALINA

The daughters of Sejanus, thrown in a dungeon were under her Aegis in effect protected. Tiberius chose for them a jailor himself. And both were dead the next day.

CALIGULA

Thanks, the advice is good in what concerns me, especially!

MESSALINA

What does Caesar mean?

CALIGULA

It's I who guard her—and that, not knowing any men in whom to confide, I don't count on giving her any other jailor. But someone is coming. That's enough. On this point, mouth shut. For we are going to have to speak of something else.

PROTOGENUS

(entering)

The orders of Caesar have been carried out.

CALIGULA

I know it.

PROTOGENUS

What more does Caesar wish?

CALIGULA

Six lictors.

PROTOGENUS

Is that enough?

CALIGULA

Yes.

PROTOGENUS

Claudius is here.

CALIGULA

Let him come in.

PROTOGENUS

Alone?

CALIGULA

No matter. Let anyone enter—but let no one leave.

MESSALINA

What's that commotion at the foot of the Palatine?

CALIGULA

Open the curtains to the pure mountain air. Heaven is radiant and the last cloud has vanished, chased by the wing of the storm.

MESSALINA

Listen, Caesar! Caesar, don't you hear?

CLAUDIUS

(entering)

Hail Caesar, do you know what's going on down there?

CALIGULA

Ah, it's you, Claudius? Heaven is propitious to you. I had you called to render me a service.

(to Claudius)

I know you are master of the art of oratory.

CLAUDIUS

Caesar flatters me.

CALIGULA

No—here it is—the Senators knowing my horse has marvelous merit came, the other day, to pay him a visit. The president then gave a long speech to this noble animal which wasn't bad. But, in default of having heard yours neither of us has been able—word of honor—to give a response. As the case can present itself again, Claudius—so in advance, Claudius, draw some good thing from your brain. I thought of Seneca but he's a true pedant, a library rat who thinks eloquence like erecting a monument is a matter of heaping up words—dust without cement.

PEOPLE

(from below)

Wheat!

CHEREA

(entering)

Hail Caesar—I've come running to get your orders. After

having committed frightful disorders the people are in tumult—assembled in the forum. Heavens! Do you hear them shout?

PEOPLE

Wheat, Caesar, wheat!

CALIGULA

By Drusilla, your sight, friend reminds me that between Muester the Slender and the Mountebank Apelles, an important debate was broached the other night—Listen, it's simply a question of knowing if, at the theater, one must with or without a harp sing the tragic verse or only speak it. Ah—there you are, Consul!

AFRANIUS

(entering, very troubled)

Yes, Caesar, yes, it's me.

CALIGULA

What's wrong you are trembling so?

AFRANIUS

I fear for you.

CALIGULA

Really!

AFRANIUS

Don't you see these senseless hordes at the foot of the Palatine, howling and shoving? Don't you hear their voices which threaten from down there?

PEOPLE

Bread, Caesar, bread.

AFRANIUS

You don't hear them?

CALIGULA

You are mistaken, Consul. They are shouts of a holiday.

AFRANIUS

Don't jest, Caesar—it's going to go to your head. Leaving the palace these furies took me without guards, without lictors and without weapons. I was not able to resist.

CALIGULA

But still. Explain—the crowd recognized your sacred majesty. Since here you are free?

AFRANIUS

Yes, but they made me take an absolute oath at their hands to bring you their rebel demands.

CALIGULA

Ah—you are coming as a herald? Your mission is beautiful. Speak!

AFRANIUS

How shall I repeat—the insolence before the Divine Emperor.

CALIGULA

Didn't you take an oath? In the book of destiny your oath is written and must be accomplished when its hour comes.

AFRANIUS

I cannot transmit such guilty vows unless Caesar orders it.

CALIGULA

Well, then I wish it.

AFRANIUS

Caesar, for the last month an unruly wind has kept the fleet from Sicily far from port—and from the shore pilots and sailors can be seen struggling vainly against the waves—so much so that the people believe they see the anger of heaven in a wind so constantly contrary—and think that Caesar must have—oh, pardon—committed some offense—it's the people speaking.

CALIGULA

Finish up!

AFRANIUS

Some offense against our gods, and that Rome is bearing for the moment the sin of a single man—so the people in their wisdom demand from Caesar an expiation.

CALIGULA

Yes, the people are right and their wisdom is great, yes, Caesar has committed a terrible fault—and Jupiter remembers an oath he made and has yet to carry out—but to repair the crime is still possible—and the expiation will be prompt and terrible.

Consul, do you recall that in Aulis the Greeks were becalmed?

The case was similar—similar the sin. Their chief had sworn to make a human sacrifice and then he thought he could, with impunity, play with Diana and betray his oath. Well, like Agamemnon I have committed a crime—a man offered himself as a sacrifice to the gods for me—and I didn't wish—weak and tender hearted—to shed this man's blood but behold the god's implacable wrath demands his blood through the people's voice. Doubtless, in acceding to it, my heart will break, but Jupiter wishes it—it is well—it shall run.

AFRANIUS

What are you saying?

CALIGULA

That Caesar is devout and that Rome must not expiate the sins of a single man.

AFRANIUS

Mercy!

PEOPLE

Bread, Caesar!

CALIGULA

Yes, people, I hear you—patience!

AFRANIUS

Caesar!

CALIGULA

Yes, in several seconds, even as the Greeks after the sacrifice saw the wind become propitious, so you will see, as soon as this man dies, our fleet return to port under full sail.

AFRANIUS

I bear the inviolable title of herald. Think carefully, Caesar, think if it!

CALIGULA

Wretch!

AFRANIUS

People—help me!

PEOPLE

The Consul! Death to Caligula! The Consul! The Consul!

CALIGULA

You want him?

(Throwing Afranius from the height of the gallery)

CALIGULA

Receive, O Jupiter, your tardy sacrifice!

CHEREA

(to Messalina)

If we can profit—

MESSALINA

(stopping him)

See—the people are falling to their knees.

PEOPLE

Glory to Caligula—Emperor without rival. Who will you give us for Consul?

CALIGULA

(with scorn)

My horse!

CURTAIN

ACT III

The atrium of Cherea's house. All around the portraits of its gods—to the left of the audience, the altar of the Lares—two side doors, a door in the rear.

CHEREA

(to his Freedman)

No one has come?

FREEDMAN

No one.

(bowing, wanting to leave)

CHEREA

Fine, stay. What time is it?

FREEDMAN

We've finished the third hour, master.

CHEREA

That's well.

FREEDMAN

My master still has need of me?

CHEREA

Yes, for I believe I can confide in you. I am going to charge you with a grave mission. Harness a chariot and go take the slave I bought last night and who is being held for me. And so that he will have no hope of escape, bind his hands and blindfold him. Then, so he won't know where he's going you will take many detours. Then bring him here.

FREEDMAN

Is he to enter this house?

CHEREA

Doubtless.

FREEDMAN

You will be satisfied, master.

CHEREA

Listen still—listen—no—nothing. Go without delay and do what I said.

(The Freedman exits.)

CHEREA

(leaning on the altar of his gods and veiling his head with his cloak)

Pardon, my gods, pardon if, speechless, mute, each time I bring my homage to your feet I veil my face with the flap of my cloak. It's because I do not raise my eyes to you, O Lares, who have seen the eyes of my ancestors. For, in looking at you, symbols of patriotism, I am ashamed to the depths of my heart for Rome and for myself who, though young, am an old soldier who saw the last hurrah of our last fine days—and of Germanicus whose memory I guard, who made me Centurion after a victory. I hope that your piercing glance has penetrated my feigned weakness and through all the detours my ruses have been forced to take— followed the lover of public glory. Oh if half my relations were known to you—-then you would have pity. Pity when you hear me speak the jargon of Ovid and Tibulus in a ridiculous voice. Pity when you see me bring my love to this Messalina, shame of our age, and pity when to the insults of the Caesar you have seen my heart cowardly submit. Well, you know, all this is only to bring my project to its bloody end. And you are aware that for it to succeed, I have had to cover it with a deep veil. Oh—doubtless in the times of ancient virtue it was not the way Brutus conspired. And it was in broad daylight that his stoic dagger avenged the Holy Republic in full Senate. But when such a project was undertaken, a friend could depose his secret in the breast of a friend without fear—for the sublime secret fell engulfed as in to an abyss. But today, soldiers, citizens, senators offer a hundred informers for a discreet friend. So much so, that when one wants a loyal and brave heart you must seek it in the breast of a slave.

O my gods! let me find in this young Gaul what I've vainly looked for a hundred times in these Roman bastards, this blind and withered race, who respond with songs to the tears of the country.

Some one's coming—Protogenus—and what has this executioner's spy come to do here?

PROTOGENUS

(entering)

Hail, Master. Here are two children that Caesar finds very disposed to become men.

(pointing to Annius and Sabinus guarded by Lictors)

Both have taken arms in hand—thinking to speak again to the old Roman people and wishing to make our Plebs believe an unheard of lie that is so ridiculous: namely that when wheat is lacking so is bread—and when bread is lacking, you will die of hunger. Happily, the crowd understood the trick and gave them up to us for justice. Therefore, the Divine Caesar, before judging them, charges you, Cherea with interrogating them—

So, you will learn from them if such ideas possess other heads. He knows your devotion—he counts on you and wants you to prove it.

CHEREA

(aside)

Does he suspect me?

PROTOGENUS

(to the two young men)

Come forward.

(to Cherea)

Fear nothing, however far your zeal carries you. Soldiers are watching at the door and I myself will remain in this place to know if I have some orders to receive from you.

(leaving with the Lictors)

CHEREA

(aside)

Yes, I understand. It's well that your fatal zeal spies at leisure on my words and deeds. Believe me, both have long been trained in the language that must be spoken before you.

(turning to the young men and recognizing them)

Annius! Sabinus!

ANNIUS

Not long ago we knew a certain Cherea, renowned in war, but we don't know any tireless actor who in peace time fills the job of inquisitor. So be it.

CHEREA

Among the jobs the Emperor dispenses under the title of favor—or for high pay—and whatever may be mine—I engage my honor that the soldier will never be shamed by the citizen.

ANNIUS

What must we think of each other?

CHEREA

Our roles are written, let's each protect our own—and so long as it does not please fate to change them, remember that mine is that of interrogator.

SABINUS

It's true by Jupiter. I'll reply to you when you've offered me a seat.

CHEREA

Take a chair. And first of all Annius what senseless demon has today thrust you into rebellion—you, the heir of a name full of glory?

ANNIUS

What suddenly flashed in my memory was one of my ancestors famous for his virtues—who died with Brutus at Phillippi.

CHEREA

And you, Sabinus?

ANNIUS

(playing with his gold chain)

I?

CHEREA

Respond.

ANNIUS

Yes, brother, respond.

SABINUS

My word, Tribune, I conspired to distract myself. For the last week, I've been so ill-treated by fate. Lepidus the best of my friends died. I sought recourse against melancholy in gambling. Gambling devoured me even to the leather of my purse to make me forget the loss of my gold. My mistress remained a last treasure. I ran to her place. An hour before my arrival the Gladiator Sergius carried her off! When this happened, the people were running amuck—I ran after them—they shouted—I shouted after them with something like "Death to Caesar", I suppose and at that moment I shouted the loudest, they captured me. I let myself be captured and I was wrong!

CHEREA

Fools that you are. You know at this game you stake both your heads against the Emperor!

ANNIUS

Each of us waits resigned. Caesar takes our heads, that's fair—he won.

CHEREA

Now must we have recourse to torture to make your confess the names of your accomplices?

SABINUS

Do what you wish.

ANNIUS

Accomplices, Tribune? As for me, I've long hoped to find one. But today hope is only a flash of light in the shadows that shivers and disappears leaving the night even darker. This man, almost a child that conquered the Marses, a simple Decurion followed Germanicus. Then as the Little Bear mounted the sky, again he followed him to Nicopolis. And, returning still followed him toward the disastrous fields, the domain of bullies where the bones of our army were blanched for six years.

Accustomed to conquer, he raised by his hand, one of those great tombs where sleep the vanished soldiers Caesar demanded of Varus.

But they tell me he's forgotten his glory since then—lost all memory of it, and traitor to himself spends his days with a courtesan in banal amours which he only leaves with great trouble to lick the hand which holds us enchained—this name once so high—and now so low, do you know him, Tribune?

CHEREA

I don't know him.

ANNIUS

That's well! May we know what fate is destined for us?

CHEREA

You will be taken to the Mamertine prison and there deploring your error, you will await the fate the clement Emperor decides.

SABINUS

Tribune—if his clemency is to be torture obtain that the executioners spare our faces, so that we won't frighten Proserpine as we enter her realm. Goodbye.

(Annius and Sabinus exit.)

CHEREA

(alone)

Goodbye, poor children, in whose fraternal souls the last fires of Republican virtue still burn—who ran very ardently towards a noble end. Not having known how to reach it, at least you will know how to die! Alas, although my heart is brother to yours—I cannot help you in the fate that awaits you.

Oh, if I had thought that in Rome there was still a bit of gold lost in our mud, I would have looked for it more carefully and at this hour of sacrifice, children, I would march as your accomplice. And at every peril prompt to participate, I would die with you instead of avenging you.

(The Freedman enters with Aquila hands bound, blindfolded.)

FREEDMAN

Master, we are here.

CHEREA

Fine, you have understood my instructions. And now, let no one come to surprise us!

FREEDMAN

Be tranquil.

(He leaves.)

(Aquila pulls off the blindfold as soon as Cherea unties his hands.)

AQUILA

Who are you?

CHEREA

Your master or your friend.

AQUILA

In that case no explanations are necessary and let's speak to each other in complete frankness.

CHEREA

Speak.

AQUILA

Victim of a crime or indeed even a mistake despite the sacred rights of Roman citizens, they've taken me, put the cords on my hands.

(throws them away)

And under the eye of a Praetor, at Rome on the banks of the Tiber been sold as a slave. And yet I was free, yes, free—I call on the gods of your house—free like the bird whose name I bear—But these affronts to which I must submit are no concern of yours—you have bought me, master. They sold you my flesh. I am nothing now. Nothing more than a man to you, your slave, your dog.

CHEREA

And so?

AQUILA

I know your rights, you can at your whim, beat me, chain me up, order my sacrifice—you can lead me to the forum, to markets with my arms crossed under the yoke. You can condemn me to infamous tortures. Load my breast with burning coals. Or, yet more cruel, place a mark on my face to externalize the affront of slavery.

Those are your rights—you see, I know the score and that I calculated your power and my shame. I have only one thing to offer you in exchange—when I wish it, I have the right to die—that alone reestablishes equality—so much so, you see, that like you, I am free.

So now, Lord, let's speak if you like citizen to citizen.

CHEREA

So be it!

AQUILA

Fix my ransom as a prisoner of war—believe me, I am no vulgar slave. And allow me to buy myself according to the contract agreed between us—in gold, horses or jewels. Look is it gold you want from me? I have enough to satisfy the most greedy souls. Alas, more than iron, gold is common among us. So set my ransom as you wish, tribune—calculated in talents not sesterces. Esteem me at the price of a satrap of Persia and if you lack time to count it, fine, we'll weigh it in your headpiece and mine.

CHEREA

Thanks.

AQUILA

I understand you. It's towards some other end than the exercise of arms that your thoughts tend. And to pay the price you believe I'm worth it will cost me ten of my most beautiful horses—in the sand their feet never leave a trace for the wind of Arabia gave them birth—which crossing Gaul Hannibal gave as a precious gift to one of my ancestors.

CHEREA

No, that's not it.

AQUILA

I see that tenderness destines my ransom to adorn your mistress. So be it. I have to complete her brilliant attractions garnet veins and shoals of coral from miners accustomed to living in the shadows who examine the sun searching for flaming carbuncles and bold divers who, under the bitter waves, pick me pearls in the depth of the seas.

CHEREA

This is still not where my supreme will tends.

AQUILA

Well then, I wait for you. Express it yourself.

CHEREA

I know that all Gauls, conquered but untamed, regret in the depths of their hearts their former liberty and like a wild horse strain impatiently at the bit of slavery. Well, it's the same, believe me, with some Romans who think the irons are too heavy to bear. And so, helping each other in their contrary fates whatever may be their countries, the oppressed are brothers.

So, one of those to whom this hope came, by chance bought an unknown slave feeling that since he was a Gaul which is to say a brave fellow he would find in him a loyal confidant, a discreet accomplice whose bold arms would powerfully aid him if he would share with him the sacred duty of delivering both Italy and Gaul from the yoke. And in this noble hope, blessed by the gods this Roman was better inspired that the one he took for his accomplice would be a slave—he could only gain his liberty (which was lost) and nothing by treason. He could, by persisting assiduously in his work, conquer for his country, or, if betrayed, die a hero.

AQUILA

And do you know the means this Roman proposes?

CHEREA

Those that a very resolved confederate will perform.

AQUILA

But still, what are they?

CHEREA

The sword and the dagger.

AQUILA

And who must he strike?

CHEREA

Caesar.

AQUILA

You see, without trembling or changing my expression, I listen to this plot formed by your courage. It's because, more than once, a similar plot has presented itself to me when I was dreaming of liberty. If when I arrived at Rome I had met a man who was involved in such a project, I would have replied simply by giving him my hand.

But since chance led the Emperor to my mother's house, where he pledged me hospitality in his wine cup and I drank with him, the ephemeral project was destroyed. I am not seduced by such high favor. But from the day Caesar became my guest even if it happened by chance—the guest is sacred. I will never kill Caesar.

CHEREA

Gaul! If this is the only way to break your chains?

AQUILA

I will die your slave.

CHEREA

This fate against which you seem to war has it not separated you from some cherished object—? Didn't you leave, in Gaul, in your distress far from you—your country, your mother, your mistress?

AQUILA

You are mistaken, tribune, at the same hour with my liberty I lost everything. The sun of my ancestors, my cherished province that I love with the burning love of patriotism. My mother who long being bound to my fate will suffer my sorrows and die my death—even my fiancée, a sweet and modest child, who was torn from me at the fatal hour, where I myself—oh—I had three noble loves and all three, I fear are lost forever which is why I offer the rest of my life to whoever would restore to me my ravished liberty.

CHEREA

Well, your liberty which you so much regret, your mistress taken from your constant love—your mother who calls you from her double widowage—your country saved from slavery—all I will return all to you if you take this dagger and if you will help me.

AQUILA

The Gods protect Caesar!

CHEREA

Gaul, aren't you afraid that now my prudence will be alarmed at this confidence I chanced to pour into your breast? Because already confirmed in my plan I can, to bring it more surely to its end, break the vase that contains it? You pray for the life of

Caesar! Think of your own.

AQUILA

Strike when you wish, Master. I belong to you.

FREEDMAN

The lady who is always accompanied by the Nubian slave wishes to speak to you immediately.

CHEREA

Let her come.

(The Freedman leaves.)

CHEREA

You go into this room for a while and you will soon know the fate which awaits you.

(Exit Aquila. Messalina enters veiled.)

CHEREA

Hail to the solitary and veiled beauty who like Phoebus on his starry route rises so radiantly on my humble horizon—and with its sweet light, brightens my house.

(raising her veil)

Allow, for a moment that on its beautiful face, the breath of love chase away this cloud and that the cherished traits blind my eyes. May the joy of a mortal render the Gods jealous?

MESSALINA

Yes, friend, but alas, tonight your faithful goddess doesn't bring pleasures with her. The entire night is not calm and serene in its course and terror seems to hunt lovers!

CHEREA

Hasn't the sedition been calmed? My queen is not alarmed over it?

MESSALINA

Oh, no—Liberty doesn't shout very long. The revolt is mute and the two leaders are taken and with that, the god's wrath is appeased to permitting vessels to enter the port of Ostia. But these dangers past another follows. And I've run, Cherea, to give you warning of it. At the time prepared for our vengeance where all those with our minds were ready, where the plot could, after many delays, break out tonight—through a sudden and un-foreseen circumstances it may be that Caesar will escape our hate.

CHEREA

Caesar escape us! Does he suspect?

MESSALINA

No. Caesar, I am certain, is still without suspicion.

CHEREA

Well—if that's the case what is there to fear? This love which you say is so troublesome to feign doesn't it still give us an easy way to enter the palace to accomplish our plans? And then

Messalina is known to the guards. Her name opens all closed doors!

MESSALINA

Yes, even yesterday that name was a talisman but since this morning there's another—and tonight perhaps the palace guard will learn to know another name.

CHEREA

What are you saying?

MESSALINA

That Caesar, changed in a single day is turned entirely toward a new amour and this feeling already has an absolute power over his soul.

CHEREA

Who is the woman who has meddled her ravishing love in our projects?

MESSALINA

A child of sixteen years, that he calls his sister. Returned two or three days ago to Baiae, unknown to me and everyone else till then—who stayed in Narbonne in Gaul and who from there was brought to Rome by a certain Aquila. You see it's some infamous conspiracy against us which we must baffle.

AQUILA

(at the door)

What's this woman saying?

MESSALINA

Despite her shouts and her tears, she was taken from her mother this morning to the palace where Caesar has hidden her—and perhaps by this evening—

AQUILA

(rushing into the room)

By the Styx—you said master, you needed a man to strike the emperor today? Here's that man. You still have it in for him?

MESSALINA

You heard us?

AQUILA

Yes.

CHEREA

You consent?

AQUILA

Right way—struck down—but by me alone—May Caesar fall and die, Tribune. Give me without delay a weapon, steel, a sword, a dagger.

CHEREA

Why from where do you get this pressing hate?

AQUILA

Don't you understand? She's my fiancée, this sister of Caesar. This young Stella—and I, I am her lover, Aquila—I who blindly brought her to Rome—to deliver her as prey to the desires of this man. For me, to save her I have only moments—quickly—a dagger—Hurry! I am waiting for you!

MESSALINA

No, Gaul—Do you believe your mistress faithful?

AQUILA

Oh—yes I believe it.

MESSALINA

Fine—then you want to be near her—I will bring you there and if you fulfill all your vows I will bring her back to your arms.

AQUILA

Can you do it?

MESSALINA

I can do it.

AQUILA

(falling on his knees)

Oh, do what you say and I, I, who in my soul worship no cult, no god—I will adore you—woman!

MESSALINA

Come along then.

AQUILA

Let's go!

CHEREA

What are you doing? When I have an accomplice so sure—

MESSALINA

I will return two to you.

(to Aquila, following her)

Come!

CURTAIN

ACT IV

A bedroom, a bed at the back. Two side doors. To the right, a window. At the head of the bed a large candelabra. At the foot of the bed a cup with lustral water. The room is surrounded with Doric columns.

STELLA

(alone, on her knees at the foot of the bed, enveloped in a large red cape—she listens with anxiety)

Didn't I hear some noise near that door? Isn't someone coming? O my God—purity or death! No, not yet—Lord of Mercy—Lord can you do less than the false gods—when fleeing from the profane pursuit of Apollo, Daphne fell dying invoking Diana—Diana heard her and with laurel bark, chaste armor, enveloped her breast. Likewise when Pan by a bold stroke was going to join Syrinx, the Arcadian, Nymph. Syrinx to escape his ravishing desires called to her aid her sisters the Naiads—and they say as soon as the fugitive nymph felt her tired feet attach to the shore and according to her desire—transformed into roses— there she mixed her last breath with the murmur of the waters. In you, then, powerful God, I confide myself and I hope that the weak find in you a second father—from Moses in the foaming Nile you heard the heavy wailing.

Your breath saved from the roaring flames the three children thrown in the burning furnace and your divine spirit descended from heaven to protect young Daniel from the lions.

My terror asks your help more than they—for they only trembled for this life, Lord, while—oh this time I am not mistaken—I hear some noise.

(rising)

They are coming.

(Running to the window.)

STELLA

At least I will escape from his infamous love, goodbye, mother, goodbye, Lord, save my soul!

AQUILA

(opens the door and raising the tapestry)

Stella!

STELLA

(rushing towards him)

My Aquila.

STELLA

(falling to her knees)

Mighty God!

AQUILA

My Stella! My love, my light, my blood!

STELLA

You have rescued me from bitter sadness. Be blessed, Lord.

(rising)

And my mother, my mother.

AQUILA

Your mother, my Stella, we will find her but first of all—we must flee.

STELLA

Do you think we can?

AQUILA

I hope so. A woman or rather a spirit having taken pity on my burning agony—through hundred obstacles, by an obscure way has led me by the hand to this door. This woman can, doubtless, unperceived escort us by the same way—and then we will flee.

STELLA

Where?

AQUILA

No matter! At chance, since we will put between us and Caesar some mountain chain or profound sea. The Alps, the ocean, or if need be—a world.

STELLA

Then not an instant to lose.

AQUILA

No—follow me.

(trying to open)

By the Styx, this door.

STELLA

It's locked?

AQUILA

Yes—see!

STELLA

Perhaps it's only difficult. And will it yield?

AQUILA

Useless! Useless! Oh, misfortune! Oh! These are your un-foreseen blows!

STELLA

But how can it be?

AQUILA

We must have been seen, and Caesar.

STELLA

Oh, be quiet—you double my fears.

AQUILA

Holds us both.

STELLA

Both?

AQUILA

And without weapons, without weapons.

STELLA

My brother, my friend, let's not despair.

AQUILA

(noticing the second door)

Yes, this door, see.

(trying to open)

Locked also.

STELLA

Alas!

AQUILA

Is there still no way out? Wait, this window—perhaps we can escape through it.

STELLA

Impossible.

AQUILA

Why not, since there are no barriers?

STELLA

Some soldiers are stationed in the courtyard.

AQUILA

Executioners! Ah—we are cursed.

STELLA

Brother!

AQUILA

No more hope.

STELLA

Brother—listen to me then—

AQUILA

Infernal suspense.

STELLA

I thought you were stronger about dying, Aquila.

AQUILA

Stella, if I had only death to fear! But before my eyes, perhaps, in the arms of this infamous one—to see you—

STELLA

Listen to me whoever wants to kill a poor weak woman like me has no need of iron—and easily can choke me with his hands—

AQUILA

What are you saying?

STELLA

Swear to me—

AQUILA

Stella.

STELLA

That the very instant that that door—

AQUILA

Enough.

STELLA

If my Aquila loves me—must he not prefer my death to dishonor?

AQUILA

Oh!

STELLA

To die by your hand would be a joy!

AQUILA

Shut up.

STELLA

Think, my Aquila.

AQUILA

This is vertigo.

STELLA

That this is the only way—the only—

AQUILA

Shut up, I tell you, shut up.

STELLA

Give him then, O mighty Jehovah, your strength—for I feel that mine is going.

(weeping)

My God, my God, to die.

AQUILA

(raising her head)

Yes, doubtless we shall die—but before dying.

STELLA

You frightened me.

AQUILA

Listen—let the last moment of our lives be entirely given over to love.

(taking her in his arms)

STELLA

(pulling away)

What are you saying? What are you doing?

AQUILA

In this supreme moment—if you love me—

STELLA

Well—finish! If I love you?

AQUILA

And if, until today your pure and virginal love was blessed by the gods—well, may this love, braving jealous death change into a spousal love. And, since we must die, Stella, no more regrets nothing but joy and annihilation after that—!

STELLA

(pulling out of his arms)

Wretch! This night that follows the light which you think is annihilation is the second life—it's the eternal day which never sets—hope for the just and the terror of the bad!

AQUILA

It's the obscure realm of funereal deities.

STELLA

O poor blind soul—full of shadows! The tomb is the barrier whereby God separates from him the unbelievers and those who adore him.

AQUILA

Well, since your God, by a barbaric law, changes error into crime—since your God separates what earth vainly attempts to bring together—then my arms come to tear you from your God!

STELLA

(inspired)

Rather his goodness will bring us together forever at the foot of his throne.

AQUILA

Together forever in heaven or a somber place wherever you like—but together.

STELLA

Oh! My God—you see—the blind opens his eyes—and in the lost shadows marches to your light.

AQUILA

But didn't you tell me?

STELLA

At the hour of death, my God will punish those who do not adore him. But for us, his justice, equal and protective, has treasures of love more than anger—and always fair, He makes eternity (like his wrath), filled with his bounty. My Aquila, my brother—listen—this very moment, you have asked me, poor fool, if I love you. Well, in this terrible and solemn moment, yes, I love you, Aquila, with an eternal love. Eternal for I want the hour of death, far from separating us, to unite as forever, oh, may the Lord inspire and second my vows—he gives me strength—hear me. I want my God to be yours, my faith to be yours. That way, in heaven, Stella will still belong to you.

AQUILA

Can it be?

STELLA

What can this moment of happiness be compared to that happiness without end which awaits above? What would be this ephemeral and guilty passion compared to the immense inexhaustible love of God—that God replaces for the other love which is no more.

AQUILA

But I am a pagan!

STELLA

What matter if your soul is ready to be lit by this celestial flame. What matter if you wish to save yourself today?

AQUILA

What has to be done to be saved?

STELLA

Believe in him.

AQUILA

Listen, I don't know if this God who inspires you will overthrow the empire of other gods—if this eternity promised to our love—was for all time or even ought to exist for a day and if from my passion the inextinguishable flame will revive in my soul after my heart dies—but, I know, in exchange, Stella that I believe all you say with your sweet voice—that I want the same blow to fall on both of us—before sharing the future of your tomb I need your night or your day to sleep here below or awake above.

STELLA

Well, then, since it pleases the Lord who sends me to lead you to heaven, friend, by this way—and that the poor woman who was a neophyte yesterday is apostle today since to show the sublime faith intention suffers where science is lacking, since He deigns to lower his divine eye on us I am going to question you.

AQUILA

I am listening to you.

STELLA

On your knees, do you believe that my God has the prolific power to make the world from nothing?

AQUILA

Yes.

STELLA

Do you believe that the Christ, predestined Savior, conceived by the Holy Spirit, was born of a Virgin?

AQUILA

Yes.

STELLA

Do you believe that through his voluntarily death, his blood has atoned the crimes of the Earth? And do you believe, he suffered and died for us—stretched on the cross? Do you believe?

AQUILA

I believe it.

STELLA

That's fine. Son, exiled from the celestial dwelling I baptize you in the name of the Holy Trinity. Shut in by ignorance and freed by faith, Christian, heaven attends you—

(seeing the door open and Caesar appear)

Martyr—arise!

AQUILA

The Emperor!

(Caesar enters with priests (Flammians) and Lictors.)

STELLA

Oh, my God—the hour has come.

CALIGULA

Oh! The cause of so much virtue is now discovered? Our modesty, the day easily frightens it but at night it thaws in the arms of another lover. I'm easy.

AQUILA

Caesar—no infamous suspicion: she's not my mistress.

CALIGULA

Then what is she?

AQUILA

My wife!

CALIGULA

Then in vain would Vesta aid her. She's your wife?

AQUILA

Yes.

CALIGULA

So much the better! She can die.

AQUILA

Die?

STELLA

(on the breast of Aquila)

Alas, my God!

AQUILA

Die—and for what crime? Because, respecting a legitimate passion she has through her sighs, her tears, her modesty repulsed the incestuous ardor of Caesar! Augustus, your ancestor, the great master of justice had put apotheosis where you put death for he remembered from Republican times the dagger of Lucretia killed Tarquin!

CALIGULA

You are mistaken, Gaul, Caesar has no hate. Caesar knows very well how to subdue a cruel fair one! He reserves the iron for Brutus—agreed! But for the Danaes he showers them with gold! If, disdaining a favor so high, this child had not committed another fault than you speak of today—she would have been honored by me and her life would have been sacred to me—but a much greater wrong makes her a criminal and it is that impiety I pursue in her.

STELLA

An impiety in me?

CALIGULA

Haven't you brought the cult of a false god from Gaul to Rome?

STELLA

You blaspheme, Caesar, he's the true God!

CALIGULA

Priests, you hear her. Take the sinner.

AQUILA

Punish me then, also—for this God is mine. And, I've been a Christian for a moment.

STELLA

Didn't I tell you that our God grows in strength?

AQUILA

Blessed be God for letting us die together!

CALIGULA

Together? No—not at all. Child, Caesar knows better than you think how to avenge the gods properly.

AQUILA

What are you saying?

CALIGULA

Someone else might have done things your way, but in torture, I am a great master.

AQUILA

Infamous!

STELLA

In the name of heaven, my Aquila, shut up!

CALIGULA

Oh—I've studied the art of executioners. And I won't commit the infinite mistake of giving you both a single agony. I know that the dying make the living suffer—and they die a thousand times watching the suffering.

STELLA

(to Aquila)

I am only a woman—fulfill my prayer.

AQUILA

What do you wish?

STELLA

Permit me to die first.

CALIGULA

Child, Caesar is good—he grants your wish—thank him!

AQUILA

Stella! Why, where is God then?

STELLA

Silence!

AQUILA

From our arms dare break the chain. Come!

CALIGULA

Lictors, separate.

(A Lictor raises his ax between the arms of the young people—Stella recoils. Aquila remains with his arms extended toward her.)

STELLA

Ah!

(The Flammians surround her and the Lictors Aquila.)

AQUILA

Demons from hell!

STELLA

Mother! Mother! Oh! Mother, name of Heaven, help us!

AQUILA

(struggling)

Stella.

CALIGULA

Secure this slave. Take this woman away.

AQUILA

Infamous!

CALIGULA

Obey!

AQUILA

Infamous!

CALIGULA

Go!

AQUILA

Infamous!

STELLA

Goodbye, my spouse! Goodbye, my mother, goodbye! We will meet again at God's side.

(The priests take Stella out through the door near the window.)

AQUILA

(bound to a column)

Your soul is avid to see tears and lamentations, Caesar. Go watch a timid woman die, for you have no one left to torture here except a man who does not know how to weep or groan.

CALIGULA

Perhaps, looking carefully we will find means with which to make this broken rock gush forth in tears.

AQUILA

Well, try it, unfeeling tiger, we'll see who will tire first, me or the executioners.

CALIGULA

Never in defiance of Caesar risk all unless you are sure of winning.

AQUILA

Well, I'm waiting.

CALIGULA

(opening the window)

Look!

AQUILA

Stella! Stella, walking to torture, Stella—before me—under my eyes, Mercy, Caligula! Mercy! Rather order that I die in her place. Oh—see like a child, I beg and I weep for those tortures I was not prepared. Oh!

CALIGULA

(laughing)

What were you saying, Gaul? I believe I have won!

(He leaves—the lictors follow him.)

AQUILA

And bound, tied, without ability to defend her, to see her—oh, this is frightful. My God—deign to hear me! My God—help us! She's coming—there, near the Lictor—! Help me! Take his ax—Stella—someone! Oh—from pity let me die with her. Help. Caesar. Phoebe—Junia.

JUNIA

(in the wings)

Who's calling me?

AQUILA

Oh mother is that you? Come—run!

JUNIA

(at the door on the right)

Here I am.

AQUILA

Where are you? Over here! Over here! Take your dagger and cut this cord right away. Cut!

(rushing to the window)

Stella!

JUNIA

(recognizing her daughter in the midst of the lictors)

Stella!

AQUILA

Too late!

JUNIA

Mercy.

(Aquila quickly shuts the window. Junia and Aquila stand immobile for a moment, without speaking then Aquila gathers the cords which have bound him. Junia drops the dagger.)

AQUILA

Bad luck to you, Caesar.

JUNIA

Back luck to you, Caesar.

AQUILA

(looking around him)

Where can we hide to kill him?

MESSALINA

(raising the tapestry at the door)

My place!

CURTAIN

ACT V

Caesar's triclinium. To the left of the spectator three beds on which lie, crowned with flowers, Caesar, having on his left Claudius and on his right the comedian Apelles—around the banqueters, young slaves dressed in white and golden belts holding in their hands purple napkins. Nymphs of Ceres to carry bread, bacchantes to pour wine—in the rear slaves circulate preceded by torches. The chamber where the scene takes place is surrounded by arcades extending back in circles.

Each arcade opens at the rise of the curtain, allowing the immense apartments of the palace to be seen. But when the curtains are shut, the room returns to the proportions of an ordinary room.

In the rear on a platform of three steps, a bed to sleep in—on both sides, two doors. To the left of the actors a tripod on which perfume is burning.

A Coryphant, lyre in hand, is on the platform.

THE CORYPHANT

(chanting)

Winter flees, perfumed Spring returns
Followed by Love and Flora

Let he who has never loved, love.
Let he who was a lover before, love again!

Winter was the sole master
When Venus came from the breast of the waves.
Her first breath gave birth to Spring
And Spring brightens the world.

Burning Summer has its mown hay,
Rich Autumn has its enclosed trellises,
Winter, its cloak of icicles,
But Spring has love and roses.

Winter flees, perfumed Spring returns
Followed by Love and Flora
Let he who has never loved, love.
Let he who was a lover before, love again!

When Venus came from the breast of the waves—her first breath gave birth to Spring, and Spring brightens the world.

MESSALINA

(dressed as a Bacchante)

Hail to Claudius the prince of the ball. Hail, Caesar—I come, Falernain in hand to plead the case of Autumn.

CALIGULA

Since, in her defense she charges Erigone we won't let her be condemned by chance. What do you say for her?

MESSALINA

Hold your cup, Caesar.

CALIGULA

(after having drunk)

Such a good pleader deserves reward.

MESSALINA

What does Caesar think now?

CALIGULA

Caesar thinks that between two seasons it's vain to choose. Spring has love, but Autumn has wine. Both have received favors without parallel so much so that to despoil the laurels and the vineyard so that with an equal ardor one would await their return—for Autumn has wine and Spring love.

MESSALINA

By Themis—this judgment is worthy of Minos. Crown Caesar with roses and vines for Bacchus and Love made him victorious and master on earth as they are in heaven.

CALIGULA

Now, Claudius, you who dispose of all, like the King of the feat invent something. You'll find us ready to second your ideas—come, Claudius, amuse us. I wish it!

CLAUDIUS

(a cup in hand)

It's wrong, Caesar to call on my wit, when near the comedian Apelles. To amuse you is his art, order him and you can punish him if he doesn't succeed.

APELLES

Caesar has only to desire it, and I am ready in a loud voice to declaim verses of Ennius or Plautus—or if Caesar chooses in his tragic ardor the sad Melpomene over her joyous sister he can choose at his taste Sophocles or Aeschylus.

CALIGULA

By Castor! Some day from Pindar to Virgil I swear to burn all these vapid writers. Even in their tombs so vain of their success. What have they done that the world should support them and think their glory equal to mine? They speak, I act. Their abortive power is only fiction. I am reality! Sometimes, by feigned dangers, they deceitfully extract tears from spectators while I, with a word inflict pain and make tears stream as I wish. Their talent would have great trouble to fill a theater while on my steps an idolatrous crowd follows me into an immense circus—where for actors I bring lions and gladiators! By a false death they frighten the guilty whereas when I'm thirsty for a real death at my feast, and with a threatening face I make death sit, an obedient banqueter, who when the hour arrives—rises to pour the poison or draw the sword.

Where are you going, Claudius?

CLAUDIUS

Caesar, it seemed to me someone was calling me in the next room.

CALIGULA

Eh! No, you're mistaken, no one is calling you. Well—what are you doing then? Aren't you drinking, Apelles? And now for wine we have some nectar to enchant Hebe!

MESSALINA

Hold your cup, Caesar!

CALIGULA

(to Apelles)

Listen—with your art, despite your usual method, I want you to make a new work! Let someone bring me those two republicans who were taken yesterday shouting "Death to the Tarquin!"

(a slave leaves)

And tomorrow in Medea or in Iphigenia you can, from them, model your death struggle.

(Cherea enters.)

CALIGULA

Ah—you here, tribune?

CHEREA

Yes, Caesar—it's my turn, tonight, to watch the palace until dawn. And I've come to ask of my august master the password.

CALIGULA

Bacchus and Cupid.

CHEREA

Perhaps the divine emperor has other commands for me?

CALIGULA

Yes, take this cup and drink. And to you who, faces wreathed in acanthus and vines; pour the sweet wine, O my beautiful bacchantes. You, nymphs of Ceres, whose golden baskets offer your fields nourishing treasures, you too, companions of Flora and Zephira who from Spring for us have pillaged her empire—while we drink let the roses of Paestum flower under your hands, they flower twice, and rock our drunkenness to the soft harmony of your songs in the Ionian cadences.

MESSALINA

(in a low voice to Cherea)

Fate, my Cherea, leads us by the hand.

CHEREA

What do you mean?

MESSALINA

All is ready.

CHEREA

For when?

MESSALINA

For tonight.

CHEREA

Then your expectation was not deceived.

MESSALINA

No. And now, all depends on your sword.

CHEREA

But the two companions, who, seconding my arms—were promised me?

MESSALINA

Wait, you will have them.

CORYPHANT

Red roses
Flower in our fields
And from the vines
Sweet raisins
Fill our baskets.

Since each year
Throwing to winter
It's faded dress
Crowned again
With green foliage.

Since all things
Offer themselves
To our disposing hand
The rose sheds its leaves
We press the grape.

For time presses us
With a steady pressure
Yesterday, youth
Tonight, old age
And tomorrow, death.

Strange mystery
Each man in his turn
Has a solitary day
On this earth
But during this day

Red roses
Flower in our fields
And from the vines
Sweet raisins
Fill our baskets.

(Annius and Sabinus are brought in dressed in black tunics, bodies wreathed with ropes and crowned with verbena.)

CALIGULA

(seeing them enter)

Change your songs of joy to funeral hymns. Here come, betrayed by contrary destinies, two Gracchi, two Bruti—unfortunate brothers who were born by misfortune fifty years too late—and who in our time had been only doubtful had they not met me on their way yesterday to repair the error committed by their fate, by advancing by fifty years their death.

ANNIUS

And why interrupt your joyous songs? Our souls are more ambitious for death than yours will ever be, these days when every hour brings its affront! When our liberty, reconquered by blood, sheds at your feet the ring of broken chains—don't go soft over our fate. Keep your most joyous songs for those who are about to die.

CALIGULA

On my soul, I find an infinite joy in seeing our wishes in such harmony. And the thing is so true, friends, that I want to grant to each the last of your vows. Ask.

SABINUS

As for me, my soul is satisfied. I got it in my head from curiosity to see, before my death, what a ferocious beast a tyrant is: to other things I'm indifferent. I saw it, at leisure, and it is, for certain, an animal that combines the tiger and hyena.

CHEREA

Wretches!

CALIGULA

Let them. The moment is not far off when—what I say you will witness—they will wish to redeem each bitter word with the lives of their sons and the blood of their mothers. But it will be too late. For my revenge on them will be terrible and without pity.

CHEREA

Wretches!

CALIGULA

(to Annius)

Now, what do you want for a last favor?

ANNIUS

A cup and some wine.

CALIGULA

I fulfill your prayer. Drink to whomever you wish, and I, without delay, will do you justice.

MESSALINA

Hold your cup, Caesar.

ANNIUS

(taking the cup and raising it above the tripod)

Pale divinities—you to whom each fall renders a tribute. All those who fall—against Caius Caesar, at this time—Hear my public denunciation, pale divinities! At the moment of death, free, I devote myself to the torments of Ixion chained to his wheel, of Tantalus, begging for water he could not touch, of Sisyphus rolling his eternal rock.

Since the same fate unites the two of us and we descend together into the same abyss.

To render without return my resolve, O Manes, receive this libation which I mix with the wine. Proceed at a feast with the funeral verbena torn from my head—in sign that I am united by a final effort—with joy even to pain and life even to death.

(pause)

Ill luck to you, Caesar. To my propitious desires. Hell, which awaits us, will receive my sacrifice.

The test is in the fire which burns more brightly.

Ill luck to you, Caesar! Ill luck to you—ill luck!

CALIGULA

(taking a knife and starting to rise from the bed)

Since the gods, towards whom your vows descend await you, Annius, let's not make them wait too long and tell them today that struck by my hand you've come to announce to them they will see me soon.

MESSALINA

(stopping)

What are you doing? Murder is too soft for such an injury. What do you keep torture for when a man insults you to this degree and can die like anyone else with a single blow without suffering?

CALIGULA

O demon of Hell! Oh! For vengeance your heart, like mine, is full of intelligence.

But which of us is worthy and who will torture them for us?

MESSALINA

(pointing to Cherea)

He will.

CHEREA

Me, Caesar?

CALIGULA

You.

CHEREA

But—

CALIGULA

Do what I order—

MESSALINA

(low to Cherea)

Take them, idiot, when Caesar gives them to you—take them, or rather before our eyes Caesar will strike them—take them—and avenge us all—do you understand?

CHEREA

(low to MESSALINA)

I understand.

(aloud)

For me, your will, Caesar, is absolute!

ANNIUS

We who are about to die, Augustus, salute you.

CALIGULA

We will see if you still keep that tone.

ANNIUS

I will try, Caesar. Meet you again—at Pluto's.

(Cherea, Annius, and Sabinus leave. Claudius has stolen out at the end of Annius's imprecation.)

CALIGULA

(standing and staggering)

Messalina!

MESSALINA

What does my August emperor desire?

MESSALINA

Messalina—wasn't their death just? Tell me.

MESSALINA

Never was an execution better deserved.

CALIGULA

No matter—I am terrified by their prayers! They say—when we are pursued by such threats, that it is necessary to make a sacrifice, there and then of relatives we love the most. Yes, I'll try it.

MESSALINA

What?

CALIGULA

Where is Claudius?

MESSALINA

Better for Caesar to wipe out in drunkenness this fatal memory the fear which presses him.

CALIGULA

No—I want Claudius. Wine is powerless to quench my thirst. Let me spill some blood.

MESSALINA

Claudius is not there!

CALIGULA

Let them find Claudius and let him die.

MESSALINA

Well, so be it, he will die—but later But now's the hour when, hair soaked by the tears of Night, Sleep, the son of the gods spreads over the earth those sweet lies that people love to believe and which open for you the ivory door. Cease to shield yourself from its powerful charm. Sleep, my noble Emperor.

CALIGULA

(falling on the bed)

Blood! Blood! Blood!

CORYPHANT

(at the head of the bed)

Caesar shuts his eyes
Day must succeed night
Which extinguishes all light
Which dissipates all noise.

Through these dark arcades
Children given to mad passions
Disappear like shadows
Flee like visions.

Go—let caprice carry you off
Each soul, according to its desire
And that, closed after you,
The gate will open only to pleasure.

(All disappear. The curtains fall.)

MESSALINA

(at the foot of the bed)

That's well! Go into the night, servile crowd and follow the lights of the orgy throughout the city. When day appears in the red orient, Caesar will have slept his last sleep—! For the guard imprudently placed at the door distracted by the noise of your senseless joy opening for pleasure has, without noticing it, allowed death to pass—toward sleeping Caesar. Come, there you are, taken in the trap. There are a double file of murderers to besiege you. And my hand is there to shut you both together—victim and murderers and will choke you all!

(Exit Messalina.)

CLAUDIUS

(coming out from behind a tapestry)

What's going to happen and what infamous feast is this woman preparing for the demons of the night? She has, I believe, spoken very guiltily in her fury of assassins threatening the life of our emperor. In striking him, what is their end, their hope? Is it another slavery? Is it deliverance? Oh—if I can flee before their attention gets to me. Bad luck! It is too late. From the alcove, noiselessly the curtain is rising—am I not in the prey of some horrible dream?

(Aquila and Junia appear during these last words—one at the foot, the other at the head of the bed.)

CLAUDIUS

No, no, it's all real.

AQUILA

(taking the lamp from its pedestal to look at Caesar.)

(replacing the lamp)

It's he!

(Aquila extends his hand toward Junia who makes a movement to strike him.)

AQUILA

Woman—wait for me.

(He places a cord around Caesar's throat, Junia places the dagger on his heart.)

JUNIA

Wake up, Caesar.

AQUILA

Caesar, wake up!

CALIGULA

(rising up)

Who calls me?

JUNIA

I do.

AQUILA

I do.

CALIGULA

Where do you get the audacity to enter here?

AQUILA

Caesar—look us in the face.

JUNIA

I—I am Junia.

AQUILA

I, I am Aquila. I am the fiancé—

JUNIA

I—the mother of Stella.

CALIGULA

What do you want at such an hour?

AQUILA

You don't know? We want to kill you.

CALIGULA

Help!

AQUILA

Like our hearts, Caesar, the walls are thick.

CALIGULA

(grabbing Junia's arm)

You are mistaken: They are coming. Help! Help!

JUNIA

(trying to get her arm free)

Bad luck!

CALIGULA

No, Jupiter does not want me to die. They are coming.

AQUILA

They are only advancing the hour of your death. That's all.

CALIGULA

Help!

JUNIA

Your shouts are useless.

CALIGULA

I am your Emperor!

AQUILA

(strangling him)

You lie. You aren't any more.

(Caligula falls and drags Aquila with him, Aquila puts his knee on Caligula's breast.)

CALIGULA

(expiring)

Ah!

AQUILA

Whoever you may be, now I defy you.

(Enter Cherea, Annius, Sabinus, sword in hand.)

Cherea, the Tribune!

CHEREA

Aquila, my slave!

ANNIUS

The Emperor.

SABINUS

The Emperor!

AQUILA

You want?

CHEREA

Yes, Caesar.

AQUILA

(pointing to the cadaver on which he is resting his foot)

I just killed him—you've come too late.

SABINUS

Dead! And not by us!

CHEREA

Friends, let's think of Rome. Our goal is attained. Honor to you, young man—honor to the man who restores us to our ancient liberty.

AQUILA

Neither from Rome nor from you have I deserved anything. Leave me.

CHEREA

My friends—before day shines we shall be masters of all.

JUNIA

Oh, my daughter, my daughter!

CHEREA

You, run to the Capitol and you run to the Senate. I will spread the word of this assassination. In the agreed way each of us will leave.

PROTOGENUS

(appearing in the doorway at right)

No one will cross the threshold of this door.

CHEREA

Who will prevent us?

(All the curtains rise—the murderers of Caesar find themselves surrounded by the German guard.)

PROTOGENUS

You see?

ANNIUS

By Jupiter—we are surrounded by a circle of iron.

CHEREA

Messalina!

PROTOGENUS

Soldier—take these criminals and hurl them from the ramparts!

CHEREA

Wretches!

(They are led off.)

SOLDIERS

Claudius! Claudius! Yes, long live Claudius!

Claudius is the only successor to Caius. The crown is here—! Tonight, during the feast—he gave us 200 diners apiece so he would be named Caesar after Caligula. Where is Claudius? Claudius!

MESSALINA

(entering and pulling the curtain which hides him)

Here he is.

CLAUDIUS

(dragged in by the soldiers)

Oh—don't kill me.

PROTOGENUS

(making him put on the gold buckler, and the first to bow before him.)

Let Caesar reign over us
And like a god, each respect and fear him.
May he be the terror and glory of the universe.

CLAUDIUS

The Empire is mine.

MESSALINA

Mine the Empire and the Emperor!

CURTAIN

ABOUT THE AUTHOR

Frank J. Morlock has written and translated many plays since retiring from the legal profession in 1992. His translations have also appeared on Project Gutenberg, the Alexandre Dumas Père web page, Literature in the Age of Napoléon, Infinite Artistries.com, and Munsey's (formerly Blackmask). In 2006 he received an award from the North American Jules Verne Society for his translations of Verne's plays. He lives and works in México.

www.ingramcontent.com/pod-product-compliance
Lightning Source LLC
LaVergne TN
LVHW041619070426
835507LV00008B/330